CHRISTIANITY|**EXPLORED**

WHAT'S THE BEST NEWS YOU'VE EVER HEARD?

LEADER'S HANDBOOK

Christianity Explored Leader's Handbook (4th Edition)

Copyright © 2016 Christianity Explored. Reprinted 2018, 2019 (twice), 2021.

www.ceministries.org

Published by:
The Good Book Company Ltd

thegoodbook.com | thegoodbook.co.uk
thegoodbook.com.au | thegoodbook.co.nz | thegoodbook.co.in

ISBN: 9781784980788 | Printed in India

Design by André Parker

WELCOME TO
CHRISTIANITY|EXPLORED

Christianity Explored is an introduction to Jesus that is grounded entirely in Mark's Gospel.

Over seven sessions, people discover the identity, mission and call of Jesus: who he is, what he achieved, and how he calls us to respond.

What makes Christianity "good news"? It's the realization that although we've rebelled against God and deserve to face his judgment, we are loved by him. Loved with an extraordinary, costly and self-sacrificing love, a love which was poured out for us on a little hill just outside Jerusalem. A love that enables us to be reconciled to God, and enjoy him forever.

Since its first publication in 2001, *Christianity Explored* has reached hundreds of thousands of people across the world, and has been translated into more than 30 languages.

Our hope is that, by God's grace, it will be of help to you too.

The Christianity Explored Team, May 2016

CONTENTS

SECTION 1
HOW TO RUN THE COURSE

Two *Christianity Explored* websites to help you:

www.christianityexplored.org
This website is for non-Christians, whether or not they are on a course. It features a visual gospel outline based on the Gospel of Mark, video answers to common questions, and testimonies from a wide variety of people, as well as information about the *Christianity Explored* course.

www.ceministries.org
For leaders looking for information, downloads and resources.

GETTING
STARTED

Telling people about Jesus Christ is a stunning privilege and a huge responsibility. It's a stunning privilege because Almighty God is pleased to call us his "fellow workers" (1 Corinthians 3:9) as he seeks and saves the lost. And it's a huge responsibility because it can be tempting to present a watered-down gospel that has no power to save and is "no gospel at all" (Galatians 1:7). Our evangelism must always be careful, prayerful and faithful.

Christianity Explored has been developed to let the Gospel tell the gospel: it takes your group members on a seven-session journey through Mark's Gospel to discover who Jesus is, what he achieved, and how he calls us to respond.

STRUCTURE OF THE COURSE

How and when you meet will depend on your situation. Many courses run on a midweek evening for seven weeks, with a day away on the Saturday between sessions 6 and 7. But your circumstances may be different.

The course material can be adapted to suit your situation, including meeting one to one with a friend or neighbour. However, you will find it helpful to meet as regularly as possible – and please don't skip any sessions or change the order. (Please use the day away material between sessions 6 and 7, even if you don't go "away" to use it.)

If this is the first time you have run *Christianity Explored*, you will find helpful tips at **www.ceministries.org**. This includes guidance on:

- setting up your venue
- choosing and training leaders
- inviting people to come

The chart below shows how the course is structured, and how the themes fit together.

	SESSION	EXPLORE (BIBLE STUDY)	LISTEN (TALK/VIDEO)	DISCUSS	FOLLOW UP (AT HOME)
IDENTITY	**Session 1: Good news** Christianity is about Christ.	Welcome	Good news	Discuss talk/video	Mark 1:1 – 3:6
IDENTITY	**Session 2: Identity** Jesus is the Christ (God's only chosen King) and God's Son.	Mark 4:35-41	Identity	Discuss talk/video	Mark 3:7 – 5:43
MISSION	**Session 3: Sin** Jesus came to cure our heart problem – our sin.	Mark 2:1-12	Sin	Discuss talk/video	Mark 6:1 – 8:29
MISSION	**Session 4: The cross** Jesus died to rescue us from sin, by taking the punishment we deserve.	Mark 8:22-33	The cross	Discuss talk/video	Mark 8:30 – 10:52

	SESSION	EXPLORE (BIBLE STUDY)	LISTEN (TALK/VIDEO)	DISCUSS	FOLLOW UP (AT HOME)
MISSION	**Session 5: Resurrection** The resurrection proves that God accepted the ransom Jesus paid, that death has been beaten, and that Jesus will come back to judge everyone.	Mark 14:27-31	Resurrection	Discuss talk/video	Mark 11:1 – 13:37
CALL	**Session 6: Grace** Jesus died to reconcile us to God, rescuing us from our sin by taking the punishment we deserve. This is grace – God's undeserved gift to us.	Mark 10:13-16	Grace	Discuss talk/video	Mark 14:1 – 16:8
CALL	**Day away** 1. The sower. We must listen to Jesus, and act on what we hear. 2. James and John. Following Jesus is about service, not status. We need to ask Jesus for mercy, not a reward. 3. King Herod. Rejecting Jesus' call to repent and believe will eventually earn us the rejection of Jesus.	Mark 4:1-9 and 13-20	The sower James and John King Herod	Discuss talk/video	
CALL	**Session 7: Come and die** A follower of Jesus "must deny himself and take up his cross". But what is given up is nothing compared to what is gained.	Mark 1:14-15	Come and die	Discuss talk/video	

The first five weeks focus on who Jesus is and what he achieved – his **identity** and **mission**. Then during the final two sessions and the day away the emphasis is on how we should respond to Jesus – his **call**. In particular, course members will explore Jesus' words in Mark 8:34: "If anyone would come after me, he must deny himself and take up his cross and follow me".

STRUCTURE OF A SESSION

Below is the suggested structure for an evening session. Of course, depending on your circumstances, you might want to change the exact times, or offer coffee and cake instead of a meal. Equally, you might want to run the course during the day if that is a more suitable time for those you're trying to reach.

6:30 p.m.	Leaders' prayer meeting
7:00 p.m.	Guests arrive for the meal
7:45 p.m.	Explore (Bible study)
8:05 p.m.	Listen (Talk/video)
8:30 p.m.	Discuss
9:00 p.m.	End of the evening – "One-to-One"

Note: All times are approximate. You can make certain sessions shorter or longer depending on your circumstances.

You can run *Christianity Explored* with Bible talks presented by the course leader or by using the course DVD or downloadable videos, presented by Rico Tice, who is Senior Minister (Evangelism) at All Souls Church, Langham Place in London.

If you decide to run the course with the talks, you can download the talk outlines from the *Christianity Explored* website. You can either download the talks as pdfs, or as Word documents so that you can adapt them for your own situation. They are available from **www.ceministries.org**.

If you decide to run the course with the DVD/videos, please note that because each episode features on-screen Bible text, it is inadvisable to use them with large groups unless you have access to a projection screen and projector.

Everyone involved in the course – leaders, guests and the course leader – will need a copy of Mark's Gospel or a Bible. It is important that everyone use the same version and edition so that page numbers will be the same. (The version used throughout the course material is the New International Version.*)

- Guests should each be given a Mark's Gospel or Bible at the beginning of the course, preferably one they can keep when the course ends.

- They should also be given a copy of the Handbook.

- Pens should be made available to allow guests to make notes or jot down questions.

---

* Note: Christianity Explored uses the 1984 edition of the New International Version (NIV). The 2011 revised edition includes a number of changes to the English text in Mark's Gospel. Where these changes involve significant words or phrases that are used within the course, there are notes in this Leader's Handbook to help you adapt the material if you are using the 2011 NIV.

BEFORE
THE COURSE

Before the course starts, there are a number of things you should do:

GET TO KNOW MARK'S GOSPEL, THE HANDBOOK AND THE VIDEOS

Read through Mark at least three times. Familiarize yourself with the Handbook that your group will be using, and the guidance on the answers to questions in the study guide section of this Leader's Handbook (page 29).

As you prepare, you might find it helpful to make notes in your copy of the group members' Handbook. Some people prefer to use an annotated Handbook to lead their group instead of referring back to this Leader's Handbook. Either way, you will feel much more confident to lead your group once you've prepared for the Bible studies and discussions.

As your group members read through Mark, you will need to be prepared to answer questions that arise from the Bible text. There is a section on page 113 that will help you prepare for these questions in advance. If, during the session, you don't know the answer to someone's question, just acknowledge the fact, and ask if you can find the answer in time for the next session.

If you are using the *Christianity Explored* DVD, or downloadable videos, watch each episode through several times. This will help you to become more familiar with the material, and also enable you to refer back to it during discussion: "Do you remember what was said in the video?"

PREPARE YOUR PERSONAL STORY

> *"Always be prepared to give an answer to everyone who asks you to give the reason for the hope that you have. But do this with gentleness and respect..."*

(1 Peter 3:15)

A personal story or testimony is an account of God's work in your life. Everybody who has been born again and who is becoming like Christ has a unique, interesting and powerful story, regardless of whether or not it appears spectacular.

At some point during the course, you may feel it appropriate to share your story with the group. Often someone will ask you directly how you became a Christian and you will need to have an answer ready.

You may find the guidelines below helpful as you prepare your story:

- Keep it honest, personal and interesting.

Tip: Your first sentence should make people sit up and listen. Anything too general, for example: "Well, I was brought up in a Christian home..." may make people switch off immediately.

- Keep it short.

Tip: Any more than three minutes may stretch people's patience. They can always ask you questions if they want to know more.

- Keep pointing to Christ, not yourself.

Tip: Your story is a great opportunity to communicate the gospel. Always include what it is that you believe, as well as how you came to believe it. As a general guide, try to explain why you think Jesus is God, how his death affects you personally, and what changes God has made in your life.

- *Prepare your personal story. (List the main points below.) You might find it useful to share your story with other leaders and get their feedback.*

_____

_____

PREPARE FOR DIFFICULT QUESTIONS

Session 1 finishes by asking the group members to answer this question: "If you could ask God one question, and you knew it would be answered, what would it be?" This will draw out a number of questions that will need careful handling. The appendices, starting on page 111, will help you deal with some of the most common questions that people may ask about Christianity in general, and about Mark's Gospel in particular.

PRAY

- that those invited will attend the course.
- that God would enable you to prepare well.
- for the logistics of organizing the course.
- for good relationships with your co-leaders and group members.
- that God would equip you to lead faithfully.
- that the Holy Spirit would open the blind eyes of those who attend.

GOD'S ROLE IN EVANGELISM
AND OURS

We need to distinguish between God's role in evangelism and our role. It's going to be incredibly frustrating if we try to fulfill God's role – because only the Creator of the universe is able to do that.

Read 2 Corinthians 4:1-6

Answer the following questions from the verses you've just read:

What is God's role in evangelism?

Why can't people see the truth of the gospel?

What is our role in evangelism?

How should we do our role in evangelism?

GOD'S ROLE IN EVANGELISM

What is God's role in evangelism? God makes "his light shine in our hearts to give us the light of the knowledge of the glory of God in the face of Christ" (2 Corinthians 4:6).

In other words, God enables us to recognize that Jesus is God. God makes it possible – by his Holy Spirit – for a person to see who Jesus is. When Paul is on the Damascus road, he asks, "Who are you, Lord?" and is told, "I am Jesus" (Acts 9:5). That is the moment of his conversion – when he recognizes for the first time who Jesus actually is.

The beginning of 2 Corinthians 4:6 reminds us that God said, "Let light shine out of darkness". That is a reference to the miracle of creation in Genesis 1:3. This same God who brought light into the world at creation now shines light into the hearts of human beings, enabling them to see that Jesus is God. In other words, for people to recognize that Jesus is God, God must perform a miracle.

People do not become Christians just because we share the gospel with them. God must shine his light in people's hearts so that they recognize and respond to the truth of the gospel.

And we know from 2 Corinthians 4:4 that people can't see the truth of the gospel because "the god of this age has blinded the minds of unbelievers".

Here, Paul reminds us that we are in the middle of a supernatural battlefield. The reason so many reject the gospel is that the devil is at work, preventing people from recognizing who Jesus is.

The devil blinds people by making them chase after the things of this world, which are passing away and which cannot save them. Their concerns are confined to the here and now: their popularity, their family, their relationships, their material possessions. They are blind to anything beyond that.

As a result, they can only see Jesus in the here and now, perhaps as a great moral teacher; his eternal significance is completely obscured. And, according to verse 4, Satan is determined to prevent people from seeing "the light of the gospel of the glory of Christ, who is the image of God". Satan does not want people to recognize who Jesus is.

OUR ROLE IN EVANGELISM

What then is our role in evangelism? "We ... preach ... Jesus Christ as Lord."

The word "preach" can evoke negative images, but it derives from a word simply meaning "herald": someone who relates important announcements from the king to his kingdom. Our role is to tell people the gospel and leave the Spirit of God to convict them of its truth.

These verses also reveal the attitude we should adopt as we preach. We are to be like "servants for Jesus' sake" (2 Corinthians 4:5). The word translated "servants" literally means "slaves" in Greek. Paul was determined to present Christ to others without any hint of self-promotion.

We must remember that the only difference between ourselves and an un-believer is that God, in his mercy, has opened our blind eyes and illuminated our hearts by his Holy Spirit. We should be forever grateful, and so seek to promote Christ, not ourselves.

We must keep preaching Christ as Lord and, remembering that only a miracle from God can open blind eyes, we must keep praying that God will shine his light in the hearts of unbelievers.

2 Corinthians 4:1-6 also helps us to carry out our role in the right way: "We do not use deception, nor do we distort the word of God ... By setting forth the truth plainly we commend ourselves to every man's conscience in the sight of God ... For we do not preach ourselves, but Jesus Christ as Lord."

When we tell people about Christ, we should demonstrate the following qual-ities:

Integrity – "We do not use deception." We are straight with people; we are genuine and sincere, and we never use any kind of emotional manipulation.

Fidelity – We do not "distort the word of God". We have to tell people the tough bits. If, for example, we don't tell people about sin, about hell, and about the necessity of repentance, then we are distorting God's word. Preach-ing these hard truths means trusting in the work of the Holy Spirit to draw people to Christ, however "difficult" the message.

Humility – "We do not preach ourselves, but Jesus Christ as Lord." We must draw people to Jesus, not to ourselves. We must remember that some people are very impressionable, and that we want them to make a decision to follow Christ because they are convinced by the truth and are being led by the Holy Spirit, rather than being manipulated by their admiration of the course leader.

As we use Christianity Explored to preach the gospel, we must remember that it is up to God whether somebody becomes a Christian or not. Only he can open blind eyes, so we must trust him for the results.

GET TO GRIPS
WITH MARK'S GOSPEL

As a *Christianity Explored* leader, it's important to familiarize yourself with Mark's Gospel before the course starts. Here's one exercise to help you do that.

Most Bibles divide Mark up with subheadings. As you finish reading each of these short sections, ask yourself: **What is this section telling me about...**

- **Jesus' Identity?** (who he is)
- **Jesus' Mission?** (what he set out to achieve)
- **Jesus' Call?** (how he's calling me to respond)

You'll find that every section of Mark's Gospel has something to say about one or more of those three themes. A great way to prepare for the course is to write "I", "M" or "C" next to each section you read.

Christianity Explored takes each theme in turn:

- Sessions 1-2 **Identity**
- Sessions 3-5 **Mission**
- Sessions 6-7 **Call**

The great drama of Mark – and *Christianity Explored* – is people's blindness to Jesus' identity, mission and call. Even those closest to Jesus repeatedly failed to see it.

The great joy of Mark – and *Christianity Explored* – is that as they spend time with Jesus, many are cured of that blindness. They come to see that Jesus is infinitely more valuable to them than anything else in the universe, and they are prepared to follow him whatever the cost.

For more on identity, mission and call in Mark's Gospel, visit **www.ceministries.org**.

For more on evangelism generally, see *Honest Evangelism* by Rico Tice with Carl Laferton.

SECTION 1 | **HOW TO RUN THE COURSE**

GETTING OUR
EXPECTATIONS RIGHT

Jesus was the most brilliant teacher who ever lived. Nevertheless, a glance through Mark chapter 3 reminds us that:

- those in authority wanted him dead (v 6).
- the public were often more interested in his miracles than in his teaching (v 9-10).
- one of his own followers would eventually betray him (v 19).
- his own family thought he was out of his mind (v 21).
- many religious people thought he was evil (v 22).

Yet, in spite of all this pressure, rather than change his approach or water down his message, Jesus continued to teach: "With many similar parables Jesus spoke the word to them, as much as they could understand" (Mark 4:33).

We, too, will face pressure. So why should we persist in teaching God's word to people who don't seem to be listening, or who openly oppose us?

Jesus gives us the answer in Mark chapter 4: God's word produces dramatic results (v 8, 20, 32). But Jesus begins by warning us to expect disappointment and delay.

EXPECT DISAPPOINTMENT

Read Mark 4:1-8, 14-20

The seed (which is "the word," as Jesus explains in v 14) can fall in unfruitful places:

- along the path (v 15)
- on rocky places (v 16)
- among thorns (v 18)

There will be those who delight us by turning up for the first session, but who never come again. There will be those who joyfully make a commitment in Session 7 but, because of family pressure, they soon decide it's just not worth the trouble. Then there are those who diligently attend each week of the course but decide right at the end that their material possessions mean more to them than anything they've heard.

It can be desperately disappointing to see group members apparently respond to the gospel message, but then show no sign of lasting change. But Jesus warns us to expect it.

EXPECT DELAY

Read Mark 4:26-29

Jesus uses the metaphor of the seed with good reason: it takes time for seed to grow.

The farmer has to be patient: "Night and day, whether he sleeps or gets up, the seed sprouts and grows, though he does not know how" (Mark 4:27). He just has to trust that the seed will grow, even though it may seem that nothing much is happening.

We live in an instant culture – instant food, instant information, instant credit – and we may find ourselves expecting guests to acquire an instant relationship with God. But delay is as much a part of our work as it is the farmer's. We must be prepared to stay in touch with group members for weeks, months, or even years after the course ends.

There will be those who seem to agree with everything they learn through the course. You decide to meet up with them on a regular basis and, a year later, they still agree with everything they've learned. But they're not Christians.

There may be times when we lose patience and are tempted to give up. But we must continue to plant the word in people's lives, trusting in its power, and remembering that God's timescale is very different from our own.

EXPECT DRAMATIC RESULTS

Read Mark 4:30-32

Despite the inevitable disappointments and delays, there is a good reason to continue sowing God's word in people's lives, just as Jesus did: "When planted, it grows and becomes the largest of all garden plants, with such big branches that the birds of the air can perch in its shade" (Mark 4:32). Even a tiny seed – like the mustard seed – can produce dramatic results.

There will be those who bring up the same difficult issues week after week. Then suddenly one of those people will arrive one week and tell you that he or she has become a Christian. A few months after that, that person is taking every opportunity to grow in their own understanding in order to be able to teach the gospel more clearly to others. And a year later that same person is a *Christianity Explored* leader.

As Jesus tells us in Mark 4:20, there will be those who hear the word, accept it, and go on to "produce a crop – thirty, sixty or even a hundred times what was sown".

It is a great encouragement to remember that the power to change lives dramatically is not in our eloquence – it is in God's word. So, whatever dis-appointments we suffer, and whatever delays we endure, keep teaching the word faithfully.

SECTION 2
STUDY GUIDE

INTRODUCTION

This study guide section contains talk outlines and studies to work through over the seven-session course. It includes all the material in the group members' Handbook. However it also contains specific instructions for leaders, additional notes and the answers to each question.

- Don't worry if you don't have time to go through all of the questions with your group – the most important thing is to listen to the guests and answer their questions.

- Try to avoid using jargon, which might alienate group members. Bear in mind that words and phrases familiar to Christians (for example, "pagan," "washed in the blood," "house group," "the Lord" and so on) may seem strange to those outside Christian circles.

- If guests miss a week, take time during the meal to summarize briefly what was taught the week before.

- Some guests may believe that the Bible is not reliable as a source of history. If this issue arises during a group discussion, refer them to the section on the reliability of Mark's Gospel on page 71 of their Handbook, or give them a copy of *Can I Really Trust The Bible?* by Barry Cooper.

SESSION 1
GOOD NEWS

- *Welcome the guests to Christianity Explored and introduce yourself. Make sure everyone has been introduced to each other. Try to remember names ready for next week.*

- *Give a brief introduction. If you have more than one discussion group, this is best given by the course leader or speaker to everyone together. (The wording below is intended only as a general guide.)*

As we begin, I want to reassure you that:

- you won't be asked to read aloud, pray, sing or do anything that makes you feel uncomfortable.

- we aren't going to take your phone number and pester you. If you decide not to come back, we are still delighted you made time to come today.

- you can ask any question you want, or alternatively feel free just to sit and listen.

Over the next seven sessions we will explore three questions that cut right to the heart of Christianity: Who is Jesus? What did he achieve? How should we respond?

We also want to spend time addressing whatever questions are important to you. As well as having times of discussion in groups, we will be available to chat at the end of the evening.

We want to give you the opportunity to encounter the real Jesus. That's why we are going to work our way through one book of the Bible, Mark's Gospel.

We want you to be able to check out the facts for yourself. That's why we will give you a reading plan that will take you right through Mark in manageable sections, so that you can examine the evidence for yourself.

Please feel free to make notes and list questions you may have as you listen to the Bible talk. There is space for notes in your Handbook.

Give each guest a Mark's Gospel or Bible and a Handbook.

Ask the group to turn to Session 1 on page 7 of the Handbook.

- Explain the four sections of the Handbook:

  Explore = we read the Bible together and talk about what we've read (different in Session 1).
  Listen = we listen to the Bible talk, or watch the video, and make notes in the talk outline in the Handbook.
  Discuss = we discuss some of the points from the Bible talk.
  Follow up = you read some of Mark for yourself; then bring any questions you have to the group.

Show the group how to find Mark in their Bibles (if you're using full Bibles), and the verse and chapter divisions, e.g. Mark 1:1 – 3:6. You may want to explain that Mark didn't divide his book into chapters and verses. These were added later to help us find our way around.

⊚ EXPLORE

Ask your group the following questions. The first one is not in the Handbook.

What's your name and what made you come on *Christianity Explored*?

This question is designed to help the group members get to know each other, and to help you begin to understand why they have come on the course.

Ask your group to turn to the question on page 7 of the Handbook.

What's the best news you've ever heard?

This question acts as an icebreaker, and also introduces the subject of "good news" before the talk/video.

⊛ LISTEN

(Page 8 in the group members' Handbook.) Encourage the group to make notes and list questions they may have as they listen to the Bible talk or watch the video. There is space in the Handbook to make notes.

"The beginning of the gospel about Jesus Christ..."

(Mark 1:1)

- When we see the order and beauty of the world and the human body, the question is: Did this all happen by chance? Or did someone create it?

- The Bible says God is the One who created the universe we live in and the bodies we inhabit. So how can we know him?

- We can know what God is like by looking at Jesus Christ.

- Christianity is about Christ – a title that means "God's only chosen King".

- Christianity is the "gospel" – the good news – about Jesus Christ.

- When Jesus was baptized, God the Father announced, "You are my Son".

- God has revealed himself in human history through Jesus Christ. When we look at Jesus, all the guessing games about God stop.

Note: Christianity Explored is based on the 1984 version of the New International Version (NIV). If you are using the 2011 revised NIV, you will find that "Jesus Christ" in Mark 1:1 has been changed to "Jesus the Messiah". The change from "Christ" to "Messiah" does not change the meaning of the verse, since the terms mean the same. They speak of the King whom God promised to send into the world. "Christ" is from the Greek word; "Messiah" comes from the Hebrew.

⬚ DISCUSS

(Page 9 in the group members' Handbook.) Ask your group if there was anything that stood out or particularly struck them from the talk/video. This will help them to respond specifically to what they have just heard, before moving on to the group discussion questions.

---

1. Is there anything that intrigues or puzzles you about Jesus?

The answers to this question will help you to get a feel for the members of your group and their current thoughts about Jesus. Don't feel that you need to comment on everything that is said. There's plenty of time for thinking to be challenged over the course of seven sessions. However, if you know that something will be looked at in a future session, do let the group members know that you will be discussing it at that point.

2. How do you feel about reading Mark's Gospel?

Have the group members understood from the talk that Christianity is about Jesus Christ, and that Mark tells us the "good news" about Jesus? This means that reading Mark's Gospel is a great way to explore Christianity.

Some of your group may be unsure or worried about reading through a whole book of the Bible. Reassure them that you will help them with any questions they have about what they've read.

3. If you could ask God one question, and you knew it would be answered, what would it be?

Ask your group to share their answers if they're happy to do so. Note down what they are so that you can deal with them at some point during the course. Do listen carefully to every question and assure your group that there will be an opportunity to return to them during *Christianity Explored*. (Some questions will be answered by the Bible studies and talks/videos and some – like questions about suffering – are best dealt with after the talks about sin or the cross.) See page 121 for guidance on common questions.

As a supplementary question, ask your group:

Think about the god you are asking that question to. What is that god like?

This will help you to get a feel for people's current views of God. You may want to refer back to some of these views later on in the course as the character of God becomes clear through his Son, Jesus.

⟶ FOLLOW UP

(Page 10 in the group members' Handbook.) Let people know that they have a section called "Follow Up" in their Handbook, which they should read through before the next session.

If you have time, show the group how to approach their personal reading plan by doing Question 1 with them. This will reassure any who are nervous about studying the Bible in this way – and will also reduce the amount of home study they need to do for this first week.

Read Mark 1:1-20

1. **The word "gospel" means "good news". Mark begins his book of good news with three statements about Jesus:**

   a) by the Old Testament prophets (messengers) (Mark 1:2-3)
   b) by John the Baptist (Mark 1:7)
   c) by God himself (Mark 1:11)

   What do they each say about Jesus?

   a) The Old Testament prophets pointed to Jesus as the Lord. They said someone would come before him to prepare the way for him.
   b) John the Baptist, himself a great prophet, said that Jesus is "more powerful" than him.
   c) God described Jesus as his own Son, whom he loves and with whom he is pleased.

Read Mark 1:21 – 2:17

2. **In chapters 1 and 2 Jesus shows his authority in different situations. (See Mark 1:16-20, 21-22, 23-28, 40-45; 2:1-12.) When Jesus speaks or acts, what sorts of things happen?**

   • He calls people, who immediately drop what they are doing and follow him (Mark 1:16-20).

   • People are astonished because he teaches with authority, and not like their religious leaders (Mark 1:21-22).

   • He rebukes evil spirits, and they leave (Mark 1:23-28).

   • He heals sickness, even the most serious illnesses (Mark 1:29-34, 40-45).

   • He forgives sins (Mark 2:1-12).

Read Mark 2:18 – 3:6

3. **Even at this early stage, Jesus divided opinions. Some people were amazed by him, while others were enraged. What are your early impressions of Jesus?**

Mark's design in writing the first part of his Gospel is to prompt the question: "Who is Jesus?". Question 3 is designed to encourage group members to reflect on what they have learned about the identity of Jesus.

Do you have any questions about Mark 1:1 – 3:6?

The next session will start with group members being asked if they have any questions about the section of Mark they read at home. You will find help in answering difficult questions from Mark's Gospel in the appendix on page 113.

SESSION 2
IDENTITY

⊚ EXPLORE

- *Ask the guests to turn to Session 2 on page 13 of the Handbook.*

- *Ask if they have any questions from last session's Follow up. The appendix on page 113 lists common questions from Mark along with suggestions for answering them.*

- *Ask everyone to open their Mark's Gospels or Bibles at Mark 4. One of the leaders should read Mark 4:35-41.*

- *Work through the questions below to help the group explore the passage.*

1. What hope of surviving the storm did the disciples have?

Almost none. The boat was "nearly swamped" (v 37). As they woke Jesus, they thought they were sure to drown (v 38).

2. What is so remarkable about the way in which Jesus calms the storm? (See Mark 4:39.)

He did it by speaking a few simple words to the forces of nature. The fact that Jesus instantly calmed not just the furious wind, but the huge waves as well — even though waves normally persist for hours after the wind dies down — shows that a miracle had taken place.

3. The verses below (from Psalm 107) were a familiar song praising God for his power over the sea. The disciples would have known it well. As you read it, look for similarities with their experience in Mark 4:35-41.

> 23 *Others went out on the sea in ships;*
> *they were merchants on the mighty waters.*
> 24 *They saw the works of the LORD,*
> *his wonderful deeds in the deep.*
> 25 *For he spoke and stirred up a tempest*
> *that lifted high the waves.*
> 26 *They mounted up to the heavens and went down to the depths;*
> *in their peril their courage melted away.*
> 27 *They reeled and staggered like drunken men;*
> *they were at their wits' end.*
> 28 *Then they cried out to the LORD in their trouble,*
> *and he brought them out of their distress.*
> 29 *He stilled the storm to a whisper;*
> *the waves of the sea were hushed.*
> 30 *They were glad when it grew calm,*
> *and he guided them to their desired haven.*
> 31 *Let them give thanks to the LORD for his unfailing love*
> *and his wonderful deeds for men.*
>
> Psalm 107:23-31

What similarities did you notice?

Group members may come up with some or all of the following. It doesn't matter if they miss one or two. The purpose is to see the close match between this Old Testament song about God, written around a thousand years before Jesus was born but sung regularly in the synagogue, and the events in Mark 4:35-41.

PSALM 107	QUOTE FROM PSALM	THE DISCIPLES' EXPERIENCE
Verse 23	"merchants on the mighty waters"	Several of the disciples had been fishermen.
Verse 24	"They saw the works of the LORD, his wonderful deeds in the deep"	The disciples saw Jesus calm the storm.
Verse 26	"They mounted up to the heavens and went down to the depths"	The furious squall threatened to sink their boat.
Verse 26	"in their peril their courage melted away"	The disciples were afraid.
Verse 27	"they were at their wits' end"	As the disciples woke Jesus, they were sure they couldn't do anything to save themselves.
Verse 28	"they cried out to the LORD in their trouble"	The disciples cried out to Jesus, although they didn't seem to expect him to be able to help.
Verses 28-29	"he brought them out of their distress. He stilled the storm to a whisper; the waves of the sea were hushed"	Jesus saved his disciples by calming both the wind and the waves.

4. The song and the story end in two different ways. (See Psalm 107:30 and Mark 4:41.) Why were the disciples still terrified after the storm had been calmed?

It is one thing to sing a praise song to God for his power over the wind and waves. It is quite another thing to be in a boat with a man who calms the sea and wind with a word – especially when seconds before you had rudely awakened him to complain that he didn't care! The awesome reality of Jesus' identity was coming home to the disciples.

(◕) LISTEN

(Page 16 in the group members' Handbook.) Encourage the group to make notes and list questions they may have as they listen to the Bible talk or watch the video. There is space in the Handbook to make notes.

"Who is this? Even the wind and the waves obey him!"

(Mark 4:41)

- It's important to get the identity of Jesus right – otherwise we'll relate to him in the wrong way.

- Mark reveals the identity of Jesus by showing:

  1. his power and authority to teach (Mark 1:21-22).
  2. his power and authority over sickness (Mark 1:29-31, 32-34, 3:22).
  3. his power and authority over nature (Mark 4:35-41; see also Psalm 107:23-31).
  4. his power and authority over death (Mark 5:21-24, 35-43).
  5. his power and authority to forgive sin (Mark 2:1-12).

- As God's Son and God's only chosen King, Jesus behaves with God's authority and displays God's power.

Note: If you are using the 2011 revised NIV, you will find that "Ignoring what they said" in Mark 5:36 has been changed to "Overhearing what they said". Changing "ignoring" to "overhearing" does not affect the overall story. The men who brought the news of the girl's death assumed there was nothing Jesus could now do. His message to Jairus, and his raising to life of the girl, show that the news of her death was no barrier to his power.

⊜ DISCUSS

(Page 17 in the group members' Handbook.) Ask your group if there was anything that stood out or particularly struck them from the talk/video. This will help them to respond specifically to what they have just heard, before moving on to the group discussion questions.

---

1. What do you think of the evidence Mark gives us?

This question will show whether group members have understood the evidence Mark has been giving for the identity of Jesus. If they only mention one or two of the five examples from the talk/video, ask specifically about the others.

2. What is your view of who Jesus is?

If some group members say they aren't sure who Jesus is, encourage them to keep reading Mark's Gospel and looking for the clues he gives us for the identity of Jesus. Some people may say that Jesus was just a particularly good teacher or a great man. If so, judge whether it would be appropriate to challenge that view, e.g. "Surely a great man wouldn't claim to be able to forgive sins".

Optional Question (if extra time):
Jesus' enemies would have looked for every opportunity to discredit him. Why didn't they do so by proving that Jesus didn't have the power and authority he claimed?

Jesus' enemies would have exposed him as a fake if they could – but there are no examples of them even trying to do this. Instead of denying his power, they claimed it came from somewhere else. Jesus had power and authority over evil spirits (e.g. Mark 1:23-28, 34; 2:10-12). The religious leaders who came from Jerusalem to investigate didn't deny this. Instead, they claimed that his power came from the devil ("Beelzebub") – an illogical claim that Jesus immediately showed to be wrong (Mark 3:22). The implication is that Jesus' enemies couldn't discredit Jesus because the evidence for his power and authority was both too strong and widely known.

If you have time, now is the moment to answer another of the questions that were asked in the first session: "If you could ask God one question, and you knew it would be answered, what would it be?" See page 121 for guidance on common questions.

⊕→ FOLLOW UP

(Page 18 in the group members' Handbook.) Ask guests to complete the following study at home, and write down any questions they have. Before the next session, look through the study yourself so that you will be able to help group members with their questions.

Read Mark 3:7 – 5:43

1. In this passage Mark records Jesus doing four specific miracles:

    a) calming a storm (Mark 4:35-41)
    b) healing a demon-possessed man (Mark 5:1-20)
    c) healing a sick woman (Mark 5:25-34)
    d) raising a dead girl to life (Mark 5:35-43)

What does Jesus show authority over in these events?

He shows authority over a) nature, b) evil spirits, c) illness and d) death.

    • How does this add to what we've already seen about his power and authority in the earlier chapters?

We have previously seen Jesus' power and authority over evil spirits and illness. In confronting nature and death itself – by calming the storm and raising a dead girl to life – Jesus shows his power and authority in new situations.

2. When Jairus's daughter died, and all hope seemed to be lost (Mark 5:35), what did Jesus ask Jairus to do (verse 36)?

He told Jairus not to be afraid, but to have faith.

• **Was that a "reasonable" thing to ask?**

Everyone else had given up, so it was an astonishing thing to ask Jairus to do. It would not have seemed "reasonable" – instead it would seem foolish and cruel. But Jesus had already shown his power and authority over nature, evil spirits and illness – and he knew that he had authority over death as well. It would seem foolish and cruel coming from anyone else, but based on Jesus' past performance, it was reasonable to ask Jairus to trust him.

3. Looking at all four events (see Question 1) what are the different ways in which people respond to Jesus? See

  a) Mark 4:40-41
  b) Mark 5:15
  c) Mark 5:27-28, 34
  d) Mark 5:42

• **Do you see yourself in any of these responses?**

a) The disciples are afraid.
b) The crowd who see him heal a demon-possessed man are afraid.
c) The woman has faith.
d) Jairus' family are amazed.

Do you have any questions about Mark 3:7 – 5:43?

The next session will start with group members being asked if they have any questions about the section of Mark they read at home. You will find help in answering difficult questions from Mark's Gospel in the appendix on page 113.

SESSION 3
SIN

⊙ EXPLORE

- *Ask the guests to turn to Session 3 on page 21 of the Handbook.*

- *Ask if they have any questions from last session's Follow up.*

- *Ask everyone to open their Mark's Gospels or Bibles at Mark 2. One of the leaders should read Mark 2:1-12.*

1. A huge crowd had gathered to hear Jesus. Why? What kind of reputation had he built up in these early days? (Look at Mark 1:27-28, 32-34, 45 for clues.)

Jesus' teaching and healing had amazed people, and news about him was spreading.

2. What were the four men hoping Jesus would do?

They must have hoped Jesus would be able to heal their friend.

3. What does Jesus do instead in Mark 2:5? Why do you think he does this first of all?

Jesus says, "Son, your sins are forgiven". That is very surprising, considering that the man was lowered through the roof to be healed, not to have his sins forgiven.

He does this first because, as we have seen (in last session's talk/video), Jesus believes that our relationship with God is far more important than our physical health. (The seriousness of sin will be the focus of today's talk/video.)

4. Why were the teachers of the law so annoyed by what Jesus said? (See Mark 2:6-7.)

Jesus was claiming to do what they believed only God can do (Mark 2:7), so they concluded that he was blaspheming.

5. Had they reached the right conclusion?

Yes and no. Yes, only God has the ultimate right and authority to forgive our sin, since all sin is an offence against God,* and all forgiveness must come from him.

No, Jesus isn't blaspheming, since as the "Son of Man" (verse 10), he has the authority of God (see next question). "Son of Man" was a title Jesus often used about himself. This title is used in other places in the Bible and refers to God's only chosen King, to whom he gives authority. (It comes from the Old Testament book of Daniel, where the Son of Man came from heaven and was given eternal rule over the whole world. See "Why did Jesus call himself the Son of Man?" in the appendix on page 114.)

* For example, although David had wronged Bathsheba's husband, Uriah, when he committed adultery with Bathsheba, he prayed, "Against you, you only, have I sinned" (Psalm 51:4). *Don't use this example unless a group member asks – it may be an unnecessary complication for the rest of the group.*

6. How do we know that Jesus has authority to forgive sin? (See Mark 2:8-12.)

He showed his authority by healing the man instantly and completely.

◉ LISTEN

(Page 24 in the group members' Handbook.) Encourage the group to make notes and list questions they may have as they listen to the Bible talk or watch the video. There is space in the Handbook to make notes.

"I have not come to call the righteous, but sinners."

(Mark 2:17)

- The reason the world is not the way it's supposed to be is because we are not the way we're supposed to be.

- Jesus tells us that "sin" comes "from within", from our "hearts" (Mark 7:20-22).

- Each of us has a heart problem. We often treat each other and our world in a shameful way, and we treat God in that way too.

- We should love God with all our heart, soul, mind and strength. But we never manage to do this.

- We've all rebelled against God, our loving Creator. The Bible calls this "sin".

- Jesus came to cure our heart problem, the problem of our sin. He came for people who realize they're bad, not for people who think they're good.

- Jesus lovingly warns us about hell because he does not want us to go there. Our sin means we're all in danger, whether we realize it or not (Mark 9:43-47).

Note: If you are using the 2011 revised NIV, you will find that throughout Mark 7:1-23 "unclean" has been changed to "defiled". The replacement of "unclean" with "defiled" is only intended to underline that this is a Jewish ceremonial issue, as verses 3-4 show. The Pharisees and teachers of the law wrongly thought it possible to be spiritually contaminated, or defiled, by contact with non-Jews. In Mark 9:42-47 "sin" has been changed to "stumble" each time. "Stumble" is probably a better translation of the Greek than "sin". But we must explain that what Jesus has in mind here is not accidental stumbling, but actual sin, which causes a moral fall.

➡ DISCUSS

(Page 25 in the group members' Handbook.) Ask your group if there was anything that stood out or particularly struck them from the talk/ video. This will help them to respond specifically to what they have just heard, before moving on to the group discussion questions.

---

1. Read Mark 9:43-47. Why do you think Jesus used such extreme language when talking about the need to avoid hell?

Jesus knows that our relationship with God is far more important than anything else. Jesus lovingly warns his disciples about hell because he does not want them to go there. Hell means eternal separation from God's blessing. Hell is the place where we face God's judgment for our rebellion against him. So we need to take this issue seriously. Hell is so serious that Jesus uses extreme examples to make his point. If we find them ridiculously extreme, it's probably because we underestimate the seriousness of the heart problem that Jesus talks about in Mark 7:14-23.

2. Jesus believed in hell. Should we? Why or why not?

If Mark's Gospel is anything to go by, Jesus is the most loving and truthful person who ever lived. Yet he spoke repeatedly about hell. That should give

SESSION 3 | **SIN**

us pause before rejecting the idea. As we'll see in the next session, hell is so serious that Jesus went through hell himself – so that we wouldn't have to.

3. Imagine that all of your thoughts, words and actions were displayed for everyone to see. How would you feel?

This question helps people to think about the detail of their own lives without them having to reveal personal issues. Hopefully it will help them to understand that everyone falls short of God's standards (in fact most will admit that they don't even meet their own standards). This means that we're all sinners – we all have a heart problem – and we all need to be rescued.

If you have time, now is the moment to answer another of the questions that were asked in the first session: "If you could ask God one question, and you knew it would be answered, what would it be?" See page 121 for guidance on common questions.

⊕ FOLLOW UP

(Page 26 in the group members' Handbook.) Ask guests to complete the following study at home, and write down any questions they have. Before the next session, look through the study yourself so that you will be able to help group members with their questions.

Read Mark 6:1 – 8:29

1. In the earlier chapters (1 – 5) Mark has built up a picture of Jesus' power and authority. He's shown us various miracles: healing the sick, casting out demons, raising the dead, calming a storm.

How does this passage (Mark 6:1 – 8:29) add to that picture? (See Mark 6:32-44, 47-48; 7:31-37; 8:1-10, 22-26.)

- Jesus is able to feed vast crowds of people from a handful of food (Mark 6:32-44; 8:1-10).

- He is able to heal the deaf and mute, and also the blind (Mark 7:31-37; 8:22-26).

- He is able to walk on water (Mark 6:47-48).

Note: The passages here are full of Old Testament imagery, pointing to the fact that Jesus is the Rescuer promised in the Old Testament. Depending on your group, it may or may not be appropriate to explain those links to them (see below*). Alternatively, you could simply mention that since the disciples (and many of the crowds) were Jewish, they would recognize echoes of the Old Testament in the things Jesus did.

* "Like sheep without a shepherd" (Mark 6:34) – In Ezekiel 34, Israel is described as being like sheep without a shepherd because her leaders had not done their job properly (Ezekiel 34:1-6). As a result, God promised to come himself to rescue his people (Ezekiel 34:16). Jesus is that rescuer, acting as God's shepherd by feeding the sheep in a miraculous way (Mark 6:30-44; 8:1-10), as God himself had done when rescuing Israel from Egypt (Exodus 16:32-35). Jesus is also said to "pass by" the disciples as he walks on water, in language reminiscent of God passing by Moses at the time he received the stone tablets (Mark 6:48; cf. Exodus 34:1-9).

2. Jesus saw the large crowd in Mark 6:34 as "sheep without a shepherd". What did he do about it?

When Jesus saw the crowd, he "had compassion on them" (v 34) and so he began to teach them.

• If Jesus looked at the faces of people in a busy town today, do you think he would feel the same? Why / why not?

The crowd in Mark 6 were Jewish, so the Jewish religious leaders should have been "shepherds" caring for them**. But most of the religious leaders failed to be the "shepherds" God wanted them to be, so this crowd were "sheep without a shepherd". In a similar way, in any crowd of people today there are likely to be many who have no clue about the good news of Jesus. Some of them may even attend church services, but have never heard the gospel message clearly explained.

** *See the note on page 54 for more on "sheep without a shepherd" (from Ezekiel 34).*

 • **Do you feel the need to have Jesus as your shepherd?**

This question is designed to encourage personal reflection.

3. Write down the very different reactions to Jesus' preaching and miracles:

   a) in his home synagogue (Mark 6:1-6)
   b) among people generally (Mark 6:14-15, 53-56; 7:37)
   c) from the disciples (Mark 6:51-52)
   d) from the religious leaders (Mark 8:11).

 • **Why do you think people responded so differently in each of these cases?**

The way people responded to Jesus seemed to be based on what they already thought about him.

a) The people from his home town, Nazareth, had seen Jesus grow up so they thought they already knew all about him. They were suspicious of him.
b) Elsewhere, Jesus had a great reputation. People had heard of his miracles and crowded to him hoping to see more of the same.
c) The disciples, who knew Jesus best, did not know what to make of him. They still didn't understand who he is.
d) The religious leaders were offended by Jesus, and wanted to "test" him. In spite of all the miracles, the Pharisees wanted him to do something spectacular – just for them.

- **Do you identify particularly with one of those groups?**

This question is designed to help group members reflect on their own response to Jesus.

4. **Read Jesus' question in Mark 8:29. How would you have answered this before you started** *Christianity Explored*?

   - **Now that you're halfway through Mark's Gospel, and have read about the amazing things that Jesus said and did, has your answer changed?**

   - **If you still have questions about the identity of Jesus, write them below.**

The three parts of question 4 are designed to encourage group members to reflect on what they have learned so far, particularly about the identity of Jesus.

Do you have any questions about Mark 6:1 – 8:29?

The next session will start with group members being asked if they have any questions about the section of Mark they read at home. You will find help in answering difficult questions from Mark's Gospel in the appendix on page 113.

SESSION 4
THE CROSS

◎ EXPLORE

- *Ask the guests to turn to Session 4 on page 29 of the Handbook.*

- *Ask if they have any questions from last session's Follow up.*

- *Ask everyone to open their Mark's Gospels or Bibles at Mark 8. One of the leaders should read Mark 8:22-33.*

1. Generally speaking, who do people today believe Jesus is? What do they base these views on?

You might ask your group to imagine that they are conducting a survey outside a popular local shop. What answers do they think they would get to the question: "Who do you think Jesus is?"

Answers are likely to be both positive and negative. They may include: a good man, a wise teacher, a prophet, a trouble-maker, a mythical person who didn't really exist…

These views can be based on things they've heard others say, the media, Sunday school, religious TV channels, etc.

2. Peter's statement in Mark 8:29 seems to form a turning point in Mark's Gospel (see Mark 8:31). What did Peter say, and why do you think it was so important?

Peter said that Jesus is the Christ (God's only chosen King). His moment of recognition was important because none of the twelve disciples had understood this so far, despite all that Jesus had said and done. Now that they recognized the identity of Jesus, he could begin to explain to them what would happen to him as God's King.

3. Once the identity of Jesus was clear (Mark 8:29), he went on to explain his mission in Mark 8:31-32. Why do you think Peter rebuked Jesus? (See Mark 8:32-33.)

Peter was appalled to hear that Jesus was willing to suffer, be rejected and die before rising again. He was driven to talk Jesus out of his mission by having in mind "the things of men", merely human priorities. This may have meant that Peter wanted Jesus to continue healing the sick and raising the dead, so that his popularity would grow. It may also have meant that Peter hoped that God's King (the Christ) would drive out the occupying Roman forces so that the country would be free.

4. Mark records the two-stage healing of the blind man in Mark 8:22-26. He went from seeing nothing (Mark 8:22) to seeing something (Mark 8:24) to seeing everything (Mark 8:25). How clearly are the disciples "seeing" the identity and mission of Jesus in Mark 8:27-33?

If your group struggle to answer this question, ask, "Peter has seen Jesus' identity in verse 29. Has he seen Jesus' mission yet?"

Peter appears to be seeing with perfect clarity in Mark 8:29 – he gets Jesus' identity right. But when Peter rebukes Jesus in verse 32, it shows that he is not seeing the nature of Jesus' mission clearly. Peter sees "something" but he is not yet seeing "everything"– so Jesus warns him, and the other disciples, not to say anything about him being the Christ (v 30).

5. Jesus told Peter he had in mind "the things of men". What phrase did Jesus use to describe his suffering and death (Mark 8:33)?

"The things of God".

   • **What does this tell us about his mission?**

Jesus was confirming that his mission came from God. It was God's plan that he would suffer and die.

6. In Mark 8:29, Jesus asks: "But what about you? Who do you say I am?" Are you able to give a definite answer to this question yet? If so, how would you answer and why?

This question is designed to reveal where the group members are in their own view of Jesus.

Rather than pressing them for an answer, it may be more appropriate for your group to reflect on this and for you to discuss it one to one later.

🔊 LISTEN

(Page 32 in the group member's Handbook.) Encourage the group to make notes and list questions they may have as they listen to the Bible talk or watch the video. There is space in the Handbook to make notes.

"For even the Son of Man did not come to be served, but to serve, and to give his life as a ransom for many."

(Mark 10:45)

• Jesus' death on a cross wasn't a tragic waste of life. It was a rescue.

• Jesus taught his followers that he must be killed. He came to "give his life as a ransom for many" (Mark 10:45).

- As Jesus was dying on the cross, darkness came over the whole land. God was acting in anger to punish sin.

- On the cross, Jesus was in some way "forsaken" or abandoned by God, as God punished sin.

- Jesus gave himself up as a substitute, to be punished on our behalf. He bore the punishment that our sin deserves, so that we can be rescued.

- When Jesus died, the curtain in the temple was torn in two from top to bottom (Mark 15:38). Because of the cross, the way is now open for people to approach God.

- The people who saw Jesus die reacted in different ways:

  1. The soldiers missed what was happening.
  2. The religious leaders were convinced they already knew the way to God.
  3. The Roman governor, Pontius Pilate, gave in to the crowd.
  4. The Roman centurion recognized the identity of Jesus: "Surely this man was the Son of God!" (Mark 15:39).

Note: If you are using the 2011 revised NIV, you will find that "two robbers" in Mark 15:27 has been changed to "two rebels". Either way, the two men crucified on either side of Jesus were rebels against the state.

🗨 DISCUSS

(Page 34 in the group members' Handbook.) Ask your group if there was anything that stood out or particularly struck them from the talk/ video. This will help them to respond specifically to what they have just heard, before moving on to the group discussion questions.

---

1. How would you feel if someone else deliberately took the punishment for something serious you had done wrong?

This question could bring out a number of reactions including:

- relieved: that you won't be punished.
- guilty: that someone has taken the blame for something they didn't do.
- bad: for the person who suffered.
- angry: that the wrong person has taken the blame for someone else's wrongdoing.
- grateful: that they've taken your punishment for you.

2. Which of the reactions to Jesus' death is most like your reaction?

Some people may not want to answer this in front of others. If no one wants to answer, you could start the conversation by asking what they think their friends might say.

This question gives an opportunity to apply the four reactions directly to people's own situations:

- The soldiers were so busy they missed what was happening right in front of them: Are we so absorbed with our busy lives that we don't take time to really think about why Jesus came, and our response to that?

- The religious leaders thought they already knew the way to God: Even if we're very "religious", none of us are good enough for God. All of us sin, and none of us can deal with our sin by ourselves. Religion can't save us. Only Jesus can.

- Pontius Pilate went with the crowd: It's very easy to give in to peer pressure. Choosing to follow Jesus would mean going his way instead of following the crowd. Are we ready to do that?

- The Roman centurion recognized who Jesus is: We don't know much about this centurion. We know he got Jesus' identity right, but we don't know what he did after that. Recognizing who Jesus is isn't all we need to do — we then need to put our trust in him to rescue us from the problem of sin and to help us live as his followers.

3. Jesus said he came "to give his life as a ransom" for sinners (Mark 10:45). What will you do with your sin?

This question aims to impress upon people the seriousness of their sin, and the need to do something about it while there's still time.

You may want to explain to your group that a "ransom" is the price paid to set a person free from something.

If you have time, now is the moment to answer another of the questions that were asked in the first session: "If you could ask God one question, and you knew it would be answered, what would it be?" See page 121 for guidance on common questions.

Give out invitations to the day away, and explain that this will be happening after Session 6 of the course. See Section 3 on page 93 for details of the day away.

⊙→ FOLLOW UP

(Page 35 in the group members' Handbook.) Ask guests to complete the following study at home, and write down any questions they have. Before the next session, look through the study yourself so that you will be able to help group members with their questions.

Read Mark 8:30 – 10:52

(Note that "Son of Man" is Jesus' way of referring to himself.)

1. Jesus directly predicts his own death and resurrection three times (Mark 8:31, 9:31 and 10:33-34). What does he say "must" and "will" happen?

He must suffer, be rejected by the religious leaders, be killed and, three days later, rise again (Mark 8:31).

He will be betrayed, killed and, three days later, rise from death (Mark 9:31).

He will be betrayed. He will be handed over to the Gentiles* by the religious leaders in Jerusalem. He will be mocked, spat on, flogged and killed. Three days later he will rise from death (Mark 10:33-34).

* In this case the "Gentiles" (non-Jews) are the Roman authorities.

2. In Mark 8:31 Jesus said he "must" die. Why did he have to die? (See Mark 10:45.)

Jesus came to serve by dying – giving his life as a ransom for many.

3. What did Jesus say that following him would mean? (See Mark 8:34.)

He said his followers must deny themselves, take up their cross and follow him.

4. Each time Jesus predicts his own death and resurrection, Mark records the disciples' response – or lack of it. (See Mark 8:32-33; 9:32-35; 10:35-45.) How do the disciples respond in each case?

Each time Jesus tells his disciples about his death, an event immediately follows that shows that the disciples have not understood his teaching:

- Peter rebukes Jesus because he hasn't understood that Jesus must suffer and die. Peter has in mind "the things of men", not of God.

- The disciples argue about who is the greatest (Mark 9:34). They haven't understood Jesus' teaching on denying themselves (Mark 8:34).

- James and John want to sit next to Jesus in his glory, because – again – they haven't learned to deny themselves and put others first.

5. In Mark 8:29 Peter recognizes that Jesus is the Christ, God's only chosen King. In taking Jesus aside and rebuking him (Mark 8:32), Peter is not treating Jesus as God's King. How do you think you have treated Jesus?

• How would you feel about Jesus being King in every area of your life?

This question is designed to help group members reflect on their own attitudes to Jesus.

Do you have any questions about Mark 8:30 – 10:52?

The next session will start with group members being asked if they have any questions about the section of Mark they read at home. You will find help in answering difficult questions from Mark's Gospel in the appendix on page 113.

SESSION 5
RESURRECTION

⊙ **EXPLORE**

- *Ask the guests to turn to Session 5 on page 39 of the Handbook.*

- *Ask if they have any questions from last session's Follow up.*

- *Ask everyone to open their Mark's Gospels or Bibles at Mark 14. One of the leaders should read Mark 14:27-31.*

1. In this section Jesus is speaking to his disciples. What predictions did Jesus make? (See Mark 14:27, 28 and 30.)

In verse 27 Jesus predicted that the disciples would all fall away (i.e. turn away from Jesus).

In verse 28 Jesus predicted that he would rise to life, and then go to Galilee (where the disciples would join him).

In verse 30 Jesus predicted that during the night, before the rooster (cockerel) crowed twice (i.e. before daybreak), Peter would disown Jesus three times.

2. In what ways does Peter disagree with Jesus' predictions? (See Mark 14:29, 31.)

In verse 29 Peter said that he would not fall away (turn away from Jesus), even if all the other disciples did.

In verse 31 Peter said that he would never disown Jesus, even if it meant dying with him.

3. In Mark 14:27 Jesus quoted from the Old Testament (Zechariah 13:7) to explain what he was about to suffer, and why the disciples would scatter. How do we know that Jesus fully intended to gather the "sheep" who would be scattered by his death? (See Mark 14:28 and Mark 16:6-7.)

We know from Mark 14:28 that Jesus was as sure about rising from death as he was about dying. We also know from Mark 16:7 that Jesus had told the disciples they would see him, alive and well, in Galilee.

4. Which of Jesus' predictions did Peter pay attention to?

• Which did he ignore?

Peter focused on Jesus' prediction that the disciples would all fall away — and insisted that he wouldn't. But he seemed to ignore what Jesus said about rising again and going ahead of them into Galilee.

5. Jesus had spoken plainly and repeatedly about his resurrection from death. (See Mark 8:31, 9:30-31, 10:32-34.) Did the disciples understand what this meant? If not, why didn't they ask Jesus about it? (See Mark 9:32.)

Mark 9:32 tells us that the disciples didn't understand what Jesus meant but were afraid to ask him about it.

The whole mission of Jesus — his rejection, suffering and death — was beyond the grasp of the disciples' minds. It was difficult for them to come to terms with these terrible aspects of his death — and even more difficult to grasp the concept of him rising from the dead.

It is important for group members to see that Mark doesn't present the resurrection as something people readily accept, but as something truly mind-blowing.

(This question is designed to draw attention to the consistency of Jesus' teaching about his resurrection – and the slowness of the disciples to come to terms with the scope of his mission. In this session we will see that, just as he said he would, Jesus rose from death (Mark 16:6-7).)

⏤ LISTEN

(Page 42 in the group members' Handbook.) Encourage the group to make notes and list questions they may have as they listen to the Bible talk or watch the video. There is space in the Handbook to make notes.

"He has risen! ... just as he told you."

(Mark 16:6-7)

- Jesus repeatedly claimed that he would be raised to life on the third day after his death.

- Jesus really did die: the women, Joseph of Arimathea, the Roman centurion and Pontius Pilate were all certain that Jesus had died.

- 36 hours later, the huge, heavy stone covering the entrance to his tomb had been rolled away.

- A young man in a white robe told the women that Jesus had risen from death. He also said that the disciples would see Jesus in Galilee, just as he had told them before he died.

- Jesus appeared to his disciples on at least ten separate occasions after his death. He also appeared to more than 500 people at the same time.

- It is not only the disciples who will see the risen Jesus. We will see him too.

- The resurrection guarantees that one day we will all be physically raised from the dead. And Jesus will be our Judge on that day.

- Jesus died to pay for sin, and rose from death to prove that sin was truly paid for. If we put our trust in Jesus, all of our sin will be fully and finally forgiven.

- Because of the resurrection, we can trust Jesus with our own death. Are we ready to meet him?

DISCUSS

(Page 43 in the group members' Handbook.) Ask your group if there was anything that stood out or particularly struck them from the talk/ video. This will help them to respond specifically to what they have just heard, before moving on to the group discussion questions.

1. **"For God has set a day when he will judge the world with justice by the man he has appointed. He has given proof of this to all men by raising him from the dead" (Acts 17:31). What's your reaction to this?**

There are two strong statements in this session that your group may find hard to believe or be unwilling to accept: that Jesus rose again, and that Jesus will return to judge everyone. The answers to this question will help you see what stage your group have reached in their responses to Jesus.

If some group members don't believe that they deserve judgment, or think they will be judged as "good", help them to understand the seriousness of sin.

If they are worried that they will "fail" the judgment, that shows they understand their heart problem – but do remind them that Jesus' death and resurrection proves that their sin, however serious, can be forgiven. Judgment is not a fearful thing for those whose trust is in the Judge. Encourage them to come to the next session to hear the good news about why God can accept us.

If group members struggle to believe/accept that Jesus will return as Judge, look again at Mark 8. Every prediction Jesus made in verse 31 came true. Is it unreasonable to believe that his prediction in verse 38 will also come true? Encourage them to read through the account again and to think about it in their own time.

If they believe everything else about Jesus up to this point, then you might like to explain that his return is logical – having conquered sin and death, he will not leave the world in its sinful struggle forever.

2. Do you believe Jesus rose from the dead? Why or why not?

This question is designed to stimulate a general discussion about the evidence as well as clarifying what the group members believe about the resurrection.

If you have time, now is the moment to answer another of the questions that were asked in the first session: "If you could ask God one question, and you knew it would be answered, what would it be?" See page 121 for guidance on common questions.

Remind the group about the day away after Session 6, and give out invitations to any who were missing last time or who have lost theirs.

⊖→ **FOLLOW UP**

(Page 44 in the group members' Handbook.) Ask guests to complete the following study at home, and write down any questions they have. Before the next session, look through the study yourself so that you will be able to help group members with their questions.

Read Mark 11:1-33

1. What is the crowd's attitude towards Jesus as he arrives in Jerusalem? (See Mark 11:8-10.)

They are respectful, joyful and hopeful – some spread their cloaks on the road; others spread branches. They welcome Jesus with shouts of praise.

Note: "Hosanna" is a Hebrew word meaning "Save us!"

2. The Old Testament prophet Zechariah wrote about a time when someone would ride into Jerusalem (also called Zion) on a colt.

> *Rejoice greatly, O Daughter of Zion!*
> *Shout, Daughter of Jerusalem!*
> *See, your king comes to you,*
> *righteous and having salvation,*
> *gentle and riding on a donkey,*
> *on a colt, the foal of a donkey.*
> (Zechariah 9:9)

What would the crowd understand about Jesus when he arrived in that way?

Zechariah prophesied about a time when Israel's King would arrive in Jerusalem (Zion). The King was righteous and had the ability to save his people. He wouldn't arrive on a war-horse, but on a colt, the foal of a donkey. So this event in Mark 11 signalled that Jesus was that King (his identity) and had come to save (his mission).

Read Mark 12:1 – 13:37

3. How do the religious leaders respond to Jesus in Mark 11:18 and 12:12?

They fear him because of his popularity with the crowd (Mark 11:18).

They look for an opportunity to arrest Jesus because they know his parable is about them and their plan to kill him (Mark 12:1-12).

4. **How do these leaders treat Jesus as a result of their fear of him? (See Mark 11:27-33; 12:13-17.)**

They question Jesus' authority.

They are two-faced: they flatter him, but seek to trap him with trick questions.

5. **The Sadducees were a group of religious leaders who did not believe in resurrection. In Mark 12:18-23 they tried to make Jesus look foolish with their question about the resurrection. What did Jesus say was the real reason for their disbelief? (See Mark 12:24.)**

Jesus said they did not know either the Scriptures (the Old Testament) or the power of God.

6. **What other criticism does Jesus make of religious leaders? (See Mark 12:38-40.)**

He talks about their pride and conceit and their hypocrisy – their concern only with appearance and reputation. They care about themselves, instead of caring for widows.

7. **A few days later the mood of the crowd had turned. Led by their religious leaders they demanded the death of Jesus (see Mark 15:9-13). Does it surprise you that it is possible to be respected, even religious, and still reject Jesus? Why or why not?**

This question will help to show whether group members have understood the difference between being religious (i.e. living a "good" life, keeping religious rules, attending church) and believing in and following Jesus.

Do you have any questions about Mark 11:1 – 13:37?

The next session will start with group members being asked if they have any questions about the section of Mark they read at home. You will find help in answering difficult questions from Mark's Gospel in the appendix on page 113.

SESSION 6
GRACE

⊚ EXPLORE

- *Ask the guests to turn to Session 6 on page 47 of the Handbook.*

- *Ask if they have any questions from last session's Follow up.*

- *Ask everyone to open their Mark's Gospels or Bibles at Mark 10. One of the leaders should read Mark 10:13-16.*

1. From all we have seen of Jesus, why do you think people would bring their children to him? (See Mark 10:13 and 16.)

They brought their children to Jesus in the hope that he would place his hands on them (v 13) and bless them (v 16).

2. We are not told why the disciples rebuked those who brought their children to Jesus. What might have been the reason for their intolerance? (See Mark 9:33-34.)

Answers may include:

- The disciples had been arguing about their own greatness. Meeting the needs of children may have been low on their priorities.

- They may have believed that Jesus was too important, busy or tired to be disturbed by "unimportant" children. (Note: Though children would have been loved by their families, they had little status in first-century Israel.)

3. Read Mark 9:33-37. In Mark 10:14 we are told that Jesus was indignant with the disciples. Are you surprised that he reacted so strongly? Why or why not?

Some may be surprised that Jesus is capable of being unashamedly indignant – but it is consistent with his love of what is good, and his appropriate anger at what is wrong.

It's not surprising that Jesus was exasperated with the disciples, since he had already given them training on welcoming children in Mark 9:35-37.

4. Read Mark 10:14-15. How do we know that Jesus is not just talking about actual children belonging to the kingdom of God?

In Mark 10:14 Jesus says that the kingdom of God (the place of God's presence and blessing) belongs to such as these. In Mark 10:15 he speaks of anyone receiving the kingdom of God like a little child. Jesus is using the children as a picture of those who receive the gift of God's kingdom.

5. Read Mark 10:16. The little children did nothing to earn acceptance by Jesus. All they did was come to him and he took them in his arms. What is the significance of this for our entry into God's kingdom? (See Mark 10:15.)

Jesus says that those who will not receive God's kingdom like little children will be unable to enter it. It is difficult for adults, who are used to having to earn acceptance with others, simply to come empty-handed to Jesus. But that is the only way into God's kingdom.

🔊 **LISTEN**

(Page 49 in the group members' Handbook.) Encourage the group to make notes and list questions they may have as they listen to the Bible talk or watch the video. There is space in the Handbook to make notes.

"I tell you the truth, anyone who will not receive the kingdom of God like a little child will never enter it."

(Mark 10:15)

- If God asked, "Why should I give you eternal life?", what would you say?

- The rich young man wanted to know how to be good enough for God.

- We can never do enough to inherit eternal life.

- Nothing we do can cure our heart problem.

- But we can receive eternal life as a free gift – paid for by the death of Jesus. This is grace – God's undeserved gift to us.

- We are more sinful than we ever realized, but more loved than we ever dreamed.

DISCUSS

(Page 50 in the group members' Handbook.) Ask your group if there was anything that stood out or particularly struck them from the talk/ video. This will help them to respond specifically to what they have just heard, before moving on to the group discussion questions.

1. "What must I do to inherit eternal life?" (Mark 10:17) How would you answer that question?

This question is designed to clarify the group's understanding of grace. There is nothing we can do, other than trust entirely in what Jesus has done. If group members still mention living a good life and doing religious things, gently point them back to Mark 10:15.

2. "You are more sinful than you ever realized, but more loved than you ever dreamed." How do you respond to this?

This question is designed to provoke reflection on these two core aspects of the gospel – hopeless human sinfulness and God's gracious love revealed in Jesus. Look out for defensive responses to the charge of personal sinfulness, which may call for a return to Mark 7:20-23.

Although it's important that the group clearly understand the hopelessness of trying to "earn" eternal life, don't end the discussion there. Emphasize the wonder of grace – God's undeserved gift to us, paid for by the death of Jesus.

3. Has grace made a difference to the view of God you had in Session 1?

This question is designed to draw out the two sides of God's character – that he is both just and merciful. God's justice means that he will not leave sin unpunished. God's mercy means that he does not treat us as we deserve, but instead he lovingly sent his Son, Jesus, to save us from our sin.

Some group members may have started this course believing that God is just a strict disciplinarian who makes rules for us to follow. Others may have seen him as automatically "welcoming everyone into heaven", except for "really bad" people. An understanding of grace will help group members to have a fuller and more biblical view of God's character.

If you have time, now is the moment to answer another of the questions that were asked in the first session: "If you could ask God one question, and you knew it would be answered, what would it be?" *See page 121 for guidance on common questions.*

Remind the group about the day away, and confirm any arrangements.

⊕ FOLLOW UP

(Page 51 in the group members' Handbook.) Ask guests to complete the following study at home, and write down any questions they have. Before the next session, look through the study yourself so that you will be able to help group members with their questions.

Read Mark 14:1-72

1. Mark tells us about Jesus' last night with his disciples, and his trial by the Jewish court, the Sanhedrin. How do we know from Mark's account that Jesus' death was not a mistake or accident? (See Mark 14:12-26, 27-31, 48-49, 61-62.)

These events show that Jesus predicted and prepared for his death. He was in total control.

- Mark 14:12-26: Jesus knew that the Passover meal would be his last meal with the disciples, and had prepared for it in advance. He also knew that one of the disciples would betray him.

- Mark 14:27-31: Jesus predicted that he would die the next day (the Passover meal was on a Thursday evening – Jesus was crucified on the Friday). He knew that the disciples would desert him, and that Peter would disown him.

- Mark 14:48-49: Jesus knew that his arrest and execution would fulfil prophecies made in the Old Testament Scriptures.

- Mark 14:61-62: Jesus knew that his death would not be the end. He would sit at the right hand of God the Father ("the Mighty One"), and return "on the clouds of heaven".

2. Jesus knew that it was his mission to die. Does that mean that death was easy for him? (See Mark 14:33-36; 15:34.)

No. Jesus' agony in the garden of Gethsemane, and his cry on the cross ("My God, my God, why have you forsaken me?") show just how hard his death was.

It's possible that a group member may say, "If Jesus' death was so hard, then surely, if God is God, there must have been another way to solve this problem". Jesus' prayer in Gethsemane answers this question decisively: "Everything is possible for you. Take this cup from me. Yet not what I will, but what you will" (Mark 14:36). The fact that Jesus' death on the cross still happened after his prayer strongly suggests that there was no other way to solve the problem: it is that serious.

Read Mark 15:1 – 16:8

3. At the moment that Jesus died, something happened in the temple on the other side of the city (Mark 15:38). What happened?

The temple curtain was torn in two from top to bottom.

> **• The temple curtain was like a big "No entry" sign. It showed that people were cut off from God because of their sins. Why do you think Mark records what happened to this curtain?**

The curtain had been a symbol of the barrier between people and God. It was torn in two as a symbol of how Jesus' death opens the way to God.

4. In Mark 14:50 we see the disciples deserting Jesus. In Mark 14:66-72 we see Peter repeatedly disowning him. Given all that Jesus had said about his death, why do you think they responded like this?

They were afraid. They didn't understand that Jesus was in control of everything that happened. They still didn't understand that Jesus had to die and rise.

5. A Roman centurion was in charge of the crucifixion. What did he say when Jesus died (Mark 15:39)?

The centurion said: "Surely this man was the Son of God!"

• **Why did he say this – and why is it surprising?**

He said this because he saw the way that Jesus died (Mark 15:37).

It is surprising because he was the Roman centurion directly responsible for Jesus' death – and yet it was his death that made clear to this man who Jesus was. (He was also a Gentile. The Jews believed that Gentiles would not be saved.)

6. Grace is when God treats us in the opposite way to what we deserve. It is an undeserved gift. Peter had disowned Jesus three times (Mark 14:66-72). How do you think Peter would have felt when he was given the message of Mark 16:7? Why?

Peter must have felt amazed to be included, and thrilled to be forgiven. He may also have been nervous about seeing Jesus.

• **The grace Jesus shows to Peter is a picture of the grace now offered to us. How will you respond to the gift Jesus offers?**

The final part of the question is designed to help group members think about their own response to all they have learned and read about God's grace.

Do you have any questions about Mark 14:1 – 16:8?

The next session will start with group members being asked if they have any questions about the section of Mark they read at home. You will find help in answering difficult questions from Mark's Gospel in the appendix on page 113.

One specific question group members may ask is why the Follow up passage ends at Mark 16:8 rather than Mark 16:20. See page 120 for a comment on Mark 16:9-20.

DAY AWAY

The day away is an important part of the *Christianity Explored* course as it will give your group members an opportunity to reflect on what they have learned and consider the implications for their own lives. The day away material is designed to be used in between Sessions 6 and 7 of the course.

The following themes will be covered:

1. The sower
We must listen to Jesus, and act on what we hear.

2. James and John
Following Jesus is about service, not status. We need to ask Jesus for mercy, not a reward.

3. Herod
Ignoring Jesus' call to repent and believe will eventually earn us the rejection of Jesus.

Spending a day together allows more time for reflection and for personal testimonies – either from leaders or other members of the church family. It will also give the group time to observe how you and your co-leaders live out your own faith in Jesus.

You will find all the material for the day away in Section 3 of this Leader's Handbook, starting on page 93.

SESSION 7
COME AND DIE

⊙ EXPLORE

- *Ask the guests to turn to Session 7 on page 65 of the Handbook.*

- *Ask if they have any questions from last session's Follow up.*

- *Ask everyone to open their Mark's Gospels or Bibles at Mark 1. One of the leaders should read Mark 1:14-15.*

1. **All through *Christianity Explored* we have heard about the good news. In Mark 1:14-15 it's mentioned twice. But to understand the good news, we need to understand the "bad news" first. What is the bad news in the following verses?**

    - **Mark 7:20-23** We are naturally sinful people and sin comes from within us.

    - **Mark 9:43-47** Sin left untreated will take us to hell.

    - **Mark 10:26-27** It is impossible for us to save ourselves from our sin.

2. **"Jesus went ... proclaiming the good news" (Mark 1:14). What is the "good news" answer to these questions from the course?**

    - **Why did Jesus come?** The good news is that Jesus came to call sinners (Mark 2:17), and to cure our heart problem by giving his life as a ransom (Mark 10:45).

- **Why did Jesus die?** The good news is that Jesus died to take the punishment we deserve, giving his life as a ransom for many. This opened up the way for us into God's presence (Mark 15:37-38).

- **Why did Jesus rise?** The good news is that Jesus is alive, having conquered death. He offers forgiveness and life after death to all who will trust him (Mark 16:6-7).

- **How can God accept us?** The good news is that what is impossible for us is possible with God (Mark 10:26-27). We can't earn our acceptance with God – it is an undeserved gift. He freely offers it to us if we come humbly, like little children, and follow Jesus (Mark 10:15).

3. **"Repent and believe the good news!" (Mark 1:15) To "repent" means to turn back in the opposite direction to the one you were travelling in. And to "believe the good news" means to act upon it, to build your life upon it. What would that mean for you?**

This is designed to provoke reflection and application of the points made in Questions 1 and 2. You may want to further explain "repent" as "to turn away from going your own way, and turn towards God and start going his way".

If the group members need prompting, you could give examples from your own life of turning back from misunderstandings about God and sin, repenting of sin, and trusting in Christ.

LISTEN

(Page 68 in the group members' Handbook.) Encourage the group to make notes and list questions they may have as they listen to the Bible talk or watch the video. There is space in the Handbook to make notes.

"If anyone would come after me, he must deny himself and take up his cross and follow me."

(Mark 8:34)

- The disciples saw Jesus' power and authority – but still asked, "Who is this?"

- Jesus healed a blind man gradually.

- The gradual healing of the man's sight reflects the gradual growth of the disciples' understanding.

- Peter sees that Jesus is the Christ, God's only chosen King.

- But the disciples' "sight" is not fully healed. Although they see who Jesus is, they don't yet see why he has come or what it means to follow him.

- Following Jesus means denying self, and taking up our cross.

- If we want to save our lives, we must entrust them to Jesus.

- A true follower of Christ is someone who clearly sees what it will cost to follow him – but does it joyfully anyway, knowing that Jesus is worth infinitely more.

- What do you see when you look at:

  - Jesus' **identity**? (Is he just a good man, or is he the Christ, the Son of God?)
  - Jesus' **mission**? (Is his death a tragic waste, or is it a rescue – a "ransom for many"?)
  - Jesus' **call**? (Is it a way of losing your life, or a way of gaining it?)

DISCUSS

(Page 69 in the group members' Handbook.) Ask your group if there was anything that stood out or particularly struck them from the talk/video. This will help them to respond specifically to what they have just heard, before moving on to the group discussion questions.

1. "What good is it for a man to gain the whole world, yet forfeit his soul?" (Mark 8:36) How would you answer that question?

This question is designed to reveal the ultimate value of the human soul, and the need to be forgiven and put right with God by trusting in Christ.

2. How might you be ashamed of Jesus and his words (Mark 8:38)?

The question is designed to help the group reflect on the reality of Jesus' call to discipleship. Answers might include:

- Embarrassment in front of friends, family and colleagues if they discovered you were a Christian.

- Unwillingness to tell others the good news about Jesus because of how they might react.

- Fear of being treated as intolerant, homophobic, stupid etc. if you stand up for what Jesus said about these and other "sensitive" areas.

3. How would you score the following statements? (0 = completely unconvinced, 10 = very sure)

Jesus is the Christ, the Son of God.

0   10

Jesus came to rescue me from my sin.

0   10

Following Jesus means denying myself and putting Jesus first, whatever the cost.

0   10

Ask the group members to put a cross on each line to score themselves from 0 to 10, using the questions above to help them. Alternatively, if they prefer, they can just write down a number for each answer.

The scores group members give themselves will help you to get a feel for where they each are in their understanding and response to the gospel message.

WHAT NOW?

Give a brief conclusion. If you have more than one discussion group, this is best given by the course leader or speaker to everyone together. (The wording below is intended only as a general guide.)

As we draw the course to a close, the natural question is: What do we do now? Although we have gone through the course as a group, we must respond personally to the good news. We are not here to put pressure on people to make commitments they are not ready to make. That would be the opposite of Jesus' example, which we have seen in Mark 8. Nevertheless, the good news does demand a response from us individually.

Let's close with that phrase of Jesus from the opening chapter of Mark.

> *"'The time has come,' he said. 'The kingdom of God is near. Repent and believe the good news!'"*
>
> (Mark 1:15)

This is a call to action. The time has come. (Let the group members feel the weight of this.)

It is not enough to know who Jesus is, what he achieved, and how he calls us to respond. We have to act on what we have come to understand – we have to respond to this good news.

There are three aspects to the command of Jesus here.

1. The kingdom of God is near

We must understand that Jesus comes to us as a conquering King. His kingdom is near. Mark has shown us the power and authority Jesus has over every other power. We have also seen that by nature we rebel against the rule of God.

How will you respond to God's King? Will you continue to resist him? Or will you gladly become his subject?

2. Repent

To live with Jesus as King involves repentance. To repent means to turn back in the opposite direction to the one you were travelling in – to turn back to God from sin. It doesn't mean we think we can live perfectly from now on – we can't. But it does mean that we face up to our personal rebellion against God and confess it to him, and seek to please him from now on.

3. Believe the good news

To believe the good news means we gladly accept and live by the fact that Jesus died for sin and rose from the dead to rescue us from it. The good news is that rebels who turn back to God by trusting in what Jesus has done for them are welcome in his kingdom forever. We know our sin no longer separates us from God.

"'The time has come,' he said. 'The kingdom of God is near. Repent and believe the good news!'"

(Mark 1:15)

How will you respond?

_____

Note to leaders: Give the group an opportunity to respond. Understandably, some may not want to talk openly, but make sure you speak to every individual before they leave, so you know best how to follow up with them. There are broadly speaking three possible responses guests could make at the end of the course:

_____

For those who are not ready to follow Jesus, but would still like to learn more, you might suggest: coming to church with you, meeting with you for one-to-one Bible study, doing the *Life Explored* course, or reading a good Christian book that addresses questions they may have. See the free download, "After the course", for help in following up group members. You can find this, and suggestions for recommended books, at **www.ceministries.org**.

For those who do not want to follow Jesus, and show no interest in taking things further: let them know how much you've valued getting to know them, and offer to meet up for a coffee in a few weeks' time if they'd like to.

For those who have heard the call to "repent and believe", and want to begin following Jesus: explain again what it means to "repent and believe".

Only God, by his Holy Spirit, can enable a person to repent and believe. "Repent" means to turn around from the direction we're currently heading in, and turn back to God. It means we start living life to please him, rather than continuing to rebel against him. "Believe" means believing that Jesus is who he says he is, and putting our trust in him as a result. It means being for what he is for, and against what he is against. As Jesus himself said, "If you love me, you will obey what I command" (John 14:15).

So to repent and believe is something that we do decisively at a moment in time, but it is not just a moment to look back on; it is a new way of life from now on. Help your group member to see what repentance and belief will look like:

- **A new attitude to God.** A follower of Jesus is deeply thankful to God, longs to know him better, love him better and be increasingly amazed by him. This longing is nurtured by reading his word, the Bible, and praying to him.

  Encourage your group member by offering to read the Bible one to one with them, and suggesting some daily Bible-reading notes. A follow-up course like *Discipleship Explored* is also a great way for a new believer to get started. (See **www.ceministries.org** for information about *Discipleship Explored*.)

  Rather than asking someone to read or repeat a prayer, encourage them to pray to God about what they've discovered on the course, thanking him for Jesus and what he means to them. Assure them that they can speak freely in their own words, because God looks into our hearts and understands our real longings – even if our words are hesitant and uncertain.

- **A new attitude to ourselves.** A follower of Jesus longs to please him by rejecting sin, and living for Jesus instead. There will be areas of our lives which we know (or will come to see) are not pleasing to him. To repent and believe means that we turn away from those ways of living, and try to live life in the way God intends. This is the life Jesus described as "life to the full" (John 10:10).

- **A new attitude to God's people.** A follower of Jesus longs to love and serve others. One way this shows itself is by committing yourself to a local church. As Jesus said, "Love one another. As I have loved you, so you must love one another. By this all men will know that you are my disciples, if you love one another" (John 13:34-35).

  Jesus commanded his followers to be baptized (Matthew 28:18-20). It's a way of publicly identifying with Christ and his people. Encourage your group member to speak to their pastor or minister about being baptized.

Offer to meet your group member at church on Sunday, and help them to establish a pattern of attending each week. Encourage them to join a small group, and to use whatever skills they have in serving their brothers and sisters in Christ.

If someone says they have repented and believed the good news, encourage them to think and behave as a believer, and to rejoice as a member of God's kingdom.

CONCLUSION

You might like to give each group member a feedback form so that you can find out what they thought of Christianity Explored (downloadable from www.ceministries.org). Assure them that their forms will be treated in confidence, and not shown to anyone else.

As you are saying goodbye to the group, however they have responded, let them know how much you've appreciated their company on the course. And do continue to pray for all your group members once the course has ended.

SECTION 3
DAY AWAY

DAY AWAY
INTRODUCTION

- *Welcome the group and thank them for coming. Give out copies of the schedule so that people know what to expect, and when the refreshment breaks will be. If you are not meeting in your usual venue, let people know where refreshments and lunch will be served, and the location of the toilets.*

- *Deliver the introduction using the notes below. These notes can also be downloaded from **www.ceministries.org** to enable you to adapt them for your group.*

Welcome to our day away together. We are delighted you have carved out the time to join us. I just want to say a word about the purpose and programme for the day.

PURPOSE

There are a couple of times in Mark where Jesus took the disciples away from the normal demands of their busy lives. He wanted to give them an opportunity to reflect on what he taught. That, in a nutshell, is the purpose of today. Mark has introduced us to the remarkable person and mission of Jesus. Today is an opportunity to get some time away; to relax and enjoy each other's company. But above all it is a time to think through the implications of what we have heard, and to discuss these things.

PROGRAMME (add your own timings)

Session 1: The Sower (Mark 4:1-9, 13-20)
We will look at one of Jesus' stories – often called "The parable of the sower". This story will remind us of the power of the gospel message – power to change our lives – and the responsibility we have to hear and receive it.

There will be a tea/coffee break at _____

Session 2: James and John (Mark 10:35-52)
Twice in this section of Mark Jesus asks, "What do you want me to do for you?" We will investigate what we think we most need in life.

We will have lunch together at _____

We then have some free time after lunch. (Let people know the options for how they can spend the free time.)

"Real lives"
Later in the afternoon we have some friends from the church coming to meet you, and to tell you a little of their journey to faith in Jesus.

There will be a tea/coffee break at _____

Session 3: Herod (Mark 6:17-29)
In our final session we will look at a king who liked to listen to a preacher. But this king chose not to act on what the preacher said, and found himself powerless over the circumstances that developed.

PS
One of those times when Jesus took the disciples away for some teaching and thinking time is recorded in Mark 9:30-32. We are told that, unfortunately, they did not understand what Jesus meant and were afraid to ask him about it. Please don't follow their example. As always, we would love to hear your thoughts and questions as we go through the day.

- *At the end of this introduction move straight on to Session 1: The sower.*

DAY AWAY 1
THE SOWER

 EXPLORE

- *Ask the group members to turn to the day away section on page 55 of the Handbook.*

- *Ask everyone to open their Mark's Gospels or Bibles at Mark 4. One of the leaders should read Mark 4:1-9 and 13-20.*

1. A parable is a story with a deeper, sometimes hidden, meaning. What does each part of this parable represent? (See Mark 4:13-20.)

The farmer represents: those who "sow the word" (Mark 4:14) i.e. those who tell people the gospel message, the good news about Jesus Christ.

The seed is: "the word" (Mark 4:14) i.e. the word of God, the Bible's message about Jesus (his identity, mission and call).

The path is like people who: hear the gospel message, but "Satan comes and takes away the word" (Mark 4:15) i.e. they hear about Jesus but quickly forget what they have heard.

The rocky soil is like those who: are full of joy at what they hear, but "last only a short time" (Mark 4:16-17) i.e. they respond well at first but fall away when trouble comes as a result of following Jesus.

What are the thorns in real life? The thorns are "the worries of this life, the deceitfulness of wealth and the desires for other things" (Mark 4:19). Ask your group what these things might be for them.

How would you recognize those who are good soil? Those who are good soil hear the gospel message, accept it and continue to be transformed by it, and live fruitful lives for God.

ⵏ LISTEN

(Page 56 in the group members' Handbook.) Encourage the group to make notes and list questions they may have as they listen to the Bible talk or watch the video. There is space in the Handbook to make notes.

"Then Jesus said, 'He who has ears to hear, let him hear.'"

(Mark 4:9)

- The good news about Jesus will only change your life if you hear it properly.

- The parable explains four different responses to the good news.

  1. Satan is like a thief who wants to take the gospel message from you.
  2. Some people give up on Jesus rather than put up with the cost of following him.
  3. Some let their desire for other things become stronger than their desire for Jesus.
  4. Some understand that Jesus is the greatest treasure in the world.

- The gospel message has the power to break through any human heart, if we will listen and act on what we hear.

⊜ DISCUSS

(Page 57 in the group members' Handbook.) Ask your group if there was anything that stood out or particularly struck them from the talk/ video. This will help them to respond specifically to what they have just heard, before moving on to the group discussion questions.

---

1. As you look back over the course, do you think some of the word has been taken from you?

If any of the group says "yes", ask them to explain what they mean. For example, someone may have missed several sessions, or have been so busy that they haven't thought about what they've heard or done any of the "Follow up" reading at home.

Group members need to be aware that Satan wants to take the gospel message from them – but do reassure them that the devil does not have the final say. Jesus has beaten Satan by his death on the cross. Encourage group members to respond properly to the things they have heard, rather than worrying about the bits they've missed.

Note: If a guest has missed a large part of the course, it may be worth encouraging them to do the course again, or offering the option of someone working through the material with them individually.

---

2. Which type of soil would you say best describes you?

This question will help group members consider what their own response has been so far to the good news about Jesus. They will be challenged further about their response in the final section of the day away.

DAY AWAY 2
JAMES AND JOHN

- *Ask the guests to turn to page 59 of the Handbook. Explain that Sessions 2 and 3 of the day away do not include an "Explore" Bible study. Instead, we will go straight into the talk/video.*

(···) LISTEN

Encourage the group to make notes and list questions they may have as they listen to the Bible talk or watch the video. There is space in the Handbook to make notes.

> *"What do you want me to do for you?"* (Mark 10:36)

- If God said, "What do you want me to do for you?", what would you ask for?

- James and John wanted power and prestige but Jesus offers something far more valuable – himself.

- Following Jesus is about service, not status.

- Contentment, satisfaction and fulfilment don't come from status-seeking, or anything else – they come from God.

- We make these things more important than God. The Bible calls this idolatry – turning something God has created into a substitute for God.

- Bartimaeus called Jesus "Son of David" and asked for mercy. He received it, and followed Jesus.

- What do you want Jesus to do for you?

🗨 DISCUSS

(Page 60 in the group members' Handbook.) Ask your group if there was anything that stood out or particularly struck them from the talk/ video. This will help them to respond specifically to what they have just heard, before moving on to the group discussion questions.

---

1. Who do you identify with most and why? James and John? Or Bartimaeus?

This question will help your group to apply the teaching from the talk/video to their own situation. If anyone says they don't identify with either James and John or with Bartimaeus, ask them to explain why.

2. What do you want Jesus to do for you?

This question is a very personal challenge for each member of the group. Encourage them to share their answers, but don't force anyone to say something if they don't want to. For some, their answer may be that they don't know what they want Jesus to do for them. If so, encourage them to keep coming to the rest of the course, and let them know that there will be further opportunities to keep exploring the message of Christianity.

The healing of Bartimaeus may have raised the issue of healing in some people's minds, in which case their answer might be that they want healing for themselves or someone else. See "Why does God allow suffering?" in the appendix on page 124 for some help in answering this question.

"REAL LIVES"

The day away provides an opportunity for others from your church or organization to serve those who have been doing the *Christianity Explored* course. For example, people who can't be regular leaders may be able to give some time to setting up the venue, serving refreshments or cooking lunch. This will give guests an opportunity to meet some other members of the church family.

One or more of these people may also be suitable to give their testimonies during the "Real lives" session in the afternoon.

PERSONAL STORIES

Choose two or three people from the church who, ideally, represent the age and gender profile of the *Christianity Explored* group. Invite them to have lunch with the group and introduce them. The most important factor in selecting these people is their ability to speak plainly and helpfully about their journey to faith in Christ and their experience of Christian living.

In the afternoon (after lunch or free time, depending on your programme) ask them to give their personal story (testimony), either directly or by interview. See page 16 for help in preparing a personal story.

Ask them to talk about:

- how they came to trust in Christ.

- the joys and struggles of Christian discipleship.

- the support they have found in the local church (e.g. small groups, one-to-one Bible reading, book and media stall etc.).

- God speaking to them as they read the Bible and hear it taught.

Check that those giving testimonies are happy to be asked questions, and encourage the *Christianity Explored* group to chat to them during the coffee break.

DAY AWAY 3
HEROD

🔊 LISTEN

(Page 61 in the group members' Handbook.) Encourage the group to make notes and list questions they may have as they listen to the Bible talk or watch the video. There is space in the Handbook to make notes.

> *"The king was greatly distressed, but because of his oaths and his dinner guests, he did not want to refuse her."*
>
> (Mark 6:26)

- We are the choices we have made.

- King Herod had John the Baptist put in prison.

- He liked to listen to John, but would not repent.

- Herod didn't act on what John said about Herodias. So in the end he felt forced to do something he didn't want to do – and had John killed.

- If we listen to Jesus, and take his words seriously, our family or friends may reject us. But there is a loving family of fellow believers who will support and encourage us.

- Though following Jesus will bring persecutions of one kind or another, Jesus promises that with them will come extraordinary blessings and joy.

- Ignoring Jesus' call to repent and believe may give us the approval of other people – but it will eventually earn us the rejection of Jesus.

🗨 DISCUSS

(Page 62 in the group members' Handbook.) Ask your group if there was anything that stood out or particularly struck them from the talk/ video. This will help them to respond specifically to what they have just heard, before moving on to the group discussion questions.

---

1. How do you think Herod felt about killing John the Baptist? (See Mark 6:20, 26, and then Mark 6:16.)

Mark 6:20 – Herod knew that John was "righteous and holy", and did not deserve the treatment he received, so he may have felt guilty. He liked to listen to John, so may have been sorry to lose that opportunity.

Mark 6:26 – Herod was distressed by the demand for John's head, but didn't want to refuse in front of his dinner guests. He didn't want to have John killed, but was caught in a trap of his own making. He may have felt he didn't have a choice – but that's not true! He could (and should) have refused the girl's request.

Mark 6:16 suggests that Herod was still thinking about John. Herod may have felt guilty for what he'd done, and perhaps worried that he was going to have to meet the man he had killed.

2. Mark tells us that "the opportune time came" (Mark 6:21). What opportunity did Herodias take? (See Mark 6:19, 24.)

Herodias had wanted to kill John the Baptist for some time (Mark 6:19), but couldn't because Herod was protecting him. Herod's foolish oath to her daughter gave Herodias the opportunity to have John "immediately" killed (Mark 6:27).

3. What opportunity did Herod miss, and why?

Herod missed the opportunity to repent: that is, to turn from what he knew was wrong, and turn back to God. He liked to listen to John, who he knew to be "a righteous and holy man" (Mark 6:20). He had heard John's clear message that his marriage to his brother's wife, Herodias, was wrong (Mark 6:18) – but had refused to repent. At the banquet Herod had the opportunity to save John's life and repent of his foolish oath to the daughter of Herodias. But he wasn't willing to do this in front of his dinner guests, so he gave the order for John's execution.

4. What kind of soil is Herod? (See Mark 4:15-20.)

Herod is the soil filled with thorns (Mark 4:18-19). He heard the word of God, taught clearly by John the Baptist, but other things choked it and made it unfruitful.

5. An old saying says, "We are the choices we have made". How was that true for Herod?

Herod had chosen to take his brother's wife and marry her. He refused to repent when John told him he was wrong. His wrong relationship with Herodias, and her hatred of John, led to Herod agreeing to John's execution. He had the opportunity to listen to God's word as spoken by John, but didn't take it. Later on, when Herod met Jesus, the opportunity had gone and Jesus didn't answer any of Herod's questions (Luke 23:9).

6. What choices will you make about the things you have heard during *Christianity Explored*?

This question is designed to challenge each group member personally about their own choices, and the implications of those.

If you have time left over at the end of this discussion, and there are any questions still unanswered from the "If you could ask God one question…" discussion in Session 1, answer them here.

• *At the end of this session move straight on to the conclusion opposite.*

DAY AWAY
CONCLUSION

Deliver the conclusion using the notes below. These notes can also be downloaded from www.ceministries.org to enable you to adapt them for your group.

As we draw the day to a close let me thank you once again for joining us. I hope you have enjoyed the opportunity to think through the implications of the good news about Jesus.

I hope you can see that to know Jesus and receive all the wonderful gifts of grace he gives – rescue, forgiveness, the Holy Spirit – we have to come to him empty handed. We can't buy or earn these things, and we can't share him with the "desires for other things" that we read about in Session 1 today. Jesus is the ultimate treasure in the universe, and in the end knowing him is all that matters.

We look forward to seeing you again on _____ at _____ for Session 7, our final time on this course. We will be looking at Mark 8: what it means to follow Jesus.

APPENDICES

QUESTIONS FROM
MARK'S GOSPEL

Mark 1:2-3
What are these strange quotes at the start?

Mark combines two quotes from the Old Testament: Malachi 3:1 and Isaiah 40:3. (It was common Jewish practice to combine two quotes, but only mention one author.) Both Malachi and Isaiah were written about 700 years before Jesus was born. The quotes promise a messenger who will one day announce the arrival of a rescuer King: the "Christ" or "Messiah", who would save God's people from judgment. This promise of a messenger is clearly fulfilled by John the Baptist in Mark 1:4-8. Even John's distinctive clothing (Mark 1:6) was like that of the Old Testament prophets, in particular Elijah (2 Kings 1:8).

Mark 1:13
What are angels?

The word literally means "messenger". They are spiritual beings in the service of God, who particularly are sent to deliver messages. An angel delivers the wonderful message of the resurrection in Mark 16:5-6. He is described as looking like a young man dressed in a white robe. No mention of wings!

Mark 1:23-27
What are evil spirits and demons?

The Bible says that there is an unseen spiritual world, which includes angels and evil spirits. According to the Bible, Satan, or the devil, is a fallen angel who is in rebellion against God and hostile to God's people. Demons are part of that fallen spiritual world, and serve Satan. Although Satan and his demons are powerful, the New Testament shows that Jesus has overcome Satan by the power of his death on the cross (see Colossians 2:15).

Note: If this topic comes up, deal with it briefly but don't allow it to dominate the session – some people are fascinated by "the dark side" and want to talk about it for hours. And make sure you explain to them that Christians have nothing to fear from the devil – Jesus has defeated him.

Mark 1:34; 7:36
Why did Jesus tell the people he healed not to tell anyone?

No one has ever healed people as Jesus did. It was instantaneous, spectacular and complete. People didn't just "start to feel a bit better". They were completely better immediately. Not surprisingly Jesus drew huge crowds who wanted to see these amazing miracles, but who seemed less interested in his teaching. Jesus did not want people coming just to see signs and wonders. He rejected such people (Mark 8:11-13). Mark 1:45 says that the result of a healed man telling everyone about his healing was that Jesus "could no longer enter a town openly but stayed outside in lonely places".

Mark 2:10
Why did Jesus call himself the Son of Man?
"Son of man" is a Jewish term meaning simply "a man". But "Son of Man" is also a well-known title used in the Old Testament for the Messiah – God's promised King. See Daniel 7:13-14. The religious leaders would have understood that when Jesus used the title "Son of Man", it was a claim to be the Messiah.

Mark 2:16
What is a Pharisee?
This group of strict Jews didn't only claim to obey the Old Testament—they invented many additional traditions to abide by. They were seen as some of the most holy men in Israel. But Jesus called them "hypocrites", which literally means "play-actors", because of their showy religiosity and self-righteousness. They looked good on the outside, but inside they lacked genuine love for God. Jesus strongly condemns them in passages such as Mark 7:6-9.

Mark 2:19
Who is the "bridegroom"?
Jesus is making the point that, for the disciples, fasting (going without food) is totally inappropriate when he's with them, just as it would be for wedding guests to be miserable at a wedding. Jesus is say-ing he is the bridegroom of God's people. This is another claim to be the Messiah promised in the Old Testament (Isaiah 54:5; 62:4-5; Hosea 2:16-20).

Mark 2:21-22
What is the new cloth/old garment, new wine/old wineskins story about?
Back in Jesus' day, goatskins were used to hold wine. While the grape juice was fermenting, it needed to be put into new wineskins which could stretch – because older, stiffer wineskins would burst. Jesus is making the point that he and his teach-ing cannot be contained by the old reli-gious forms.

Mark 2:23
What is the Sabbath?
The Sabbath was the special day of rest when no work was done. The Sabbath was an opportunity for God's people to remember God's creation and how he res-cued them from Egypt.

Mark 3:6
Who are the Herodians?
These were supporters of Herod Antipas, the ruler of Galilee and Perea. Like the Pharisees, they would have seen Jesus as a threat to their power.

Mark 3:13-19
Why did Jesus choose twelve apostles?
Jesus calls the twelve apostles on a mountainside. In the Old Testament God shows himself to his people on mountains (e.g. Genesis 8; Exodus 19; and 1 Kings 18). There were twelve tribes of Israel – God's people in the Old Testament. Jesus is making the point that God is calling a new group of people to follow him.

Mark 3:22

What does it mean to be possessed by Beelzebul?

Beelzebul is another name for the devil. Note that the religious authorities don't question whether Jesus is powerful or whether the miracles happen; they simply question the source of his power. Their accusation is that his power to drive out demons comes from the devil. Jesus points out that their claim is foolish (Mark 2:23-27): if the "prince of demons" really was driving out other demons, then he would be fighting against himself.

Mark 3:29

What is the blasphemy against the Holy Spirit that will never be forgiven?

The religious leaders have seen Jesus perform wonderful miracles, and have heard his astonishing teaching. Now they claim that the work of the Holy Spirit is actually the work of the devil. Jesus' warning has nothing to do with swearing at the Holy Spirit. In simple terms, it means rejecting the only way of forgiveness that God has provided. Of course, this sin is only unforgivable for as long as a person goes on committing it. Many of the same religious leaders changed their minds about Jesus later, and so were forgiven (Acts 6:7). This is vital to understand: there can be no forgiveness if we finally reject Jesus, because we are rejecting the only way of forgiveness that God has provided.

Mark 4:2

Why did Jesus teach in parables?

Jesus answers this question in Mark 4:10-12 (see also Matthew 13:10-17; 34-35). His teaching has two effects: as the old saying goes, "The same sun that melts wax also hardens clay". On the one hand, to those who reject him, Jesus' teaching "hardens". Because they've rejected him, they find that the spiritual truth in parables is hidden from them. On the other hand, to those who accept him, Jesus' teaching "reveals". Because they've accepted him, they find that previously hidden things in parables are revealed to them: "The secret of the kingdom of God has been given to you" (Mark 4:11).

Mark 4:40

Why does Jesus say, "Do you still have no faith?"

Despite all the evidence they've seen, the disciples still don't have faith in Jesus. (Note: to "have faith" in someone means to trust him or her.) The disciples express terror rather than trust both before and after Jesus acts. Interestingly, just before this miracle, Jesus has told three parables making the point that God's word is powerful. He then calms the storm with a word. The disciples should have drawn the obvious conclusion.

Mark 6:3

Did Jesus have brothers and sisters?

These were the natural children of Joseph and Mary, conceived after the birth of Jesus. See also Mark 3:32. This answers the question as to whether Mary remained a virgin after the birth of Jesus. In addition, Matthew 1:25 certainly implies that Joseph and Mary had a normal sexual relationship after Jesus was born.

Mark 6:7-11

Why did Jesus send out the twelve disciples?

Jesus sends out the twelve disciples, telling them to expect some to accept and some to reject their message. They are to reject those who, by refusing to listen, reject them. The reference to shaking off dust refers to what Jews did on returning to Israel from Gentile countries, which they viewed as "unclean". For the disciples to do it in a Jewish village was like calling the village Gentile! It is a mark of judgment (see also Acts 13:51).

Mark 6:14-29
Why is there all this stuff about John the Baptist?

Mark tells us about the death of John the Baptist to make an important point. It answers the question that is implied in Mark 6:1-13: why don't people see who Jesus is? The answer is that people reject Jesus because, like Herod, they will not repent. In other words, they will not turn from their rebellion against God.

Mark 7:24-30
Why does Jesus call this woman a dog?

This incident shows that Jesus saves Gentiles as well as Jews. The woman is a Gentile (a non-Jew) from near the city of Tyre. "Children" here refers to the Jews, and "dogs" was an unflattering expression that Jews used for any Gentile person. So Jesus is saying, "It isn't right to take what belongs to the Jews and give it to you Gentiles". In her reply (v 28) the woman is saying, "Yes Lord – I acknowledge that as a Gentile woman I have no right to ask help from you, the Jewish Messiah. But you have such great power and mercy that you must have enough to help me as well!" Jesus is impressed by her faith and her persistence, and grants her request.

Mark 8:15
What is the yeast of the Pharisees and Herod?

Yeast – what we put in bread to make it rise – is used as a picture in the New Testament to refer to the influence of someone or something. Just as a tiny amount of yeast has a great effect on the whole batch of dough, so Jesus warns against being affected by the sinful attitudes of the Pharisees and Herod: specifically, hypocrisy and worldliness.

Mark 8:17-21
Why do the disciples not understand?

Jesus has fed thousands in the desert (twice), healed people, forgiven sin, cast out evil spirits and stilled storms with a word. So what's wrong with the disciples? Why can't they see who Jesus is? As the following two stories show, they need spiritual help to understand the truth that is staring them in the face. Spiritual truth can only be revealed by God's Spirit. They need a miracle in order to "see" who Jesus is, just as the blind man at Bethesda (Mark 8:22-25) needed a miracle.

Mark 8:22-25
Why is there a two-part healing?

Jesus hasn't lost his touch, or found it difficult to heal this man. He is doing the healing as a kind of "acted parable", to explain what happens next. When Peter announces that Jesus is "the Messiah" in Mark 8:29, he is like the man in Mark 8:24 (he has partial sight). It is clear from the verses that follow – where Peter rebukes Jesus – that although he has understood who Jesus is, he has not yet realized why Jesus has come (Mark 8:30-33).

Mark 8:32-33

Why does Jesus say: "Get behind me, Satan!"?

Peter had recognized that Jesus was the Christ, but he could not understand why Jesus had to suffer and die. Jesus recognizes in Peter's words a temptation to reject God's plan that the Christ should die on the cross. It is not that Peter is Satan, or that Satan has "taken control". It is just that Peter is saying what the devil wants, which is to knock Jesus off course in his mission to rescue us by dying on the cross and rising to life again.

Mark 9:1

What does Jesus mean when he says that some "will not taste death before they see that the kingdom of God has come with power"?

This probably refers to the transfiguration of Jesus, recorded immediately after (Mark 9:2-7), although it could also be a reference to the coming of the Holy Spirit on the Day of Pentecost (Acts 1:8).

Mark 9:4

Who are Elijah and Moses?

Both of these people represent the Old Testament: Moses was the law-giver and Elijah the greatest of the Old Testament prophets. The fact that they talk with Jesus shows that he is the one the Old Testament is pointing to.

Mark 9:11-13

What does Jesus mean when he says, "Elijah does come first"?

The disciples have failed to recognize that John the Baptist was the Elijah-like messenger promised in Malachi 4:5-6 who would come before "the Lord". Elijah was a prophet in the eighth century BC who lived out in the wilderness, wearing animal skins and a leather belt (2 Kings 1:8). This is how John the Baptist is described in Mark 1:6. Jesus makes it clear that John was the fulfilment of the prophecy concerning Elijah.

Mark 9:43-48

Why does Jesus tell us to cut our hands off?

Jesus obviously did not intend that a Christian should physically cut off a hand or foot, or pluck out an eye. It's not as if sin is confined to a particular part of our bodies. Jesus is making this point: "If anything is stopping you from entering the kingdom of God, it is better to take drastic action to rid yourself of it, whatever it is, than to end up in hell forever." The logic is clear: temporary pain is better than eternal punishment.

Mark 10:1-12

What does Jesus think about divorce?

Jesus makes it clear that divorce is always against the perfect purpose of God. God's plan in creation is that married people should live together for their whole lives (see Genesis 2:24). Jesus says that if people seek a divorce because they have found an alternative partner, such action is adultery (Mark 10:11-12). It is only because people's hearts are so hard (Mark 10:5) that divorce could ever be permitted. The danger is either that we use the concession of verse 5 as an excuse for deliberate sin, or that we think that divorce cuts us off from God forever. Christ came to die for all sin, including the failures of divorce.

Note: Be aware that you are likely to have people in your group who have experienced the reality of broken marriages. For some this may be a significant personal issue.

Mark 10:15
What does it mean to "receive the kingdom of God like a little child"?

The disciples need to understand that they have nothing to offer God, and must therefore depend fully on God, just as a little child depends fully on its parents. Jesus is not implying that children are innocent or pure – neither of which are traits of most children!

Mark 10:38
What did Jesus mean when he said, "Can you drink the cup I drink?"

In the Old Testament, "the cup" was generally a reference to suffering. It also refers to the cup of God's anger (see Jeremiah 25:15-16). In Mark 10:38, Jesus is showing that the disciples don't know what they are talking about. They, unlike Jesus, have their own sin to deal with and therefore cannot suffer God's wrath on other people's behalf; a sinless substitute is required. However, Jesus adds – in verse 39 – that they will suffer.

Mark 11:12-14, 20-21
Why did Jesus curse the fig-tree?

This can seem strange as it is Jesus' only destructive miracle. Mark interweaves the cursing of the fig-tree with the events in the temple (Mark 11:15-19, 27-33). In the same way that Jesus curses the fig-tree for having no fruit on it, he condemns the "fruitlessness" of Israel's religion (i.e. the lack of genuine worship, the failure to recognize Jesus as the Messiah, etc.).

Mark 12:1-12
What does the story about the vineyard mean?

This parable is very similar to Isaiah 5, where the people of Israel are rebuked for the terrible way in which they have rejected God, and are told that God's righteous judgment will come. Jesus' hearers would have understood that the "man" who owns the vineyard is God; the tenants of the vineyard are the religious leaders and people of Israel; and the son (who the tenants kill) is Jesus.

Mark 12:10
What is a capstone?

This is the most important stone; the foundation stone. Here it means that although Israel's leaders have rejected Jesus, he is still the Messiah, and will become the Saviour through dying on the cross.

Mark 12:18-27
What's the point of the strange "one bride for seven brothers" story?

In Jesus' day there were two major religious groups who disagreed about what would happen to people after they died. The Pharisees believed in resurrection after death. The Sadducees said that death was the end. So the Sadducees came up with this question to try and show that the resurrection of the dead was a ridiculous idea. In his answer, Jesus makes two things clear. First, that there is indeed life after death for God's people. He reminds the Sadducees that in the Old Testament, God refers to himself as "the God of Abraham, the God of Isaac and the God of Jacob". Because God is the God of the living, not the dead, Abraham, Isaac and Jacob must still be living. Second, Jesus makes it clear that we shouldn't think of life after death as though it were exactly the same as this life, just with the bad bits taken out. There will be significant differences. One difference is that people will not marry or be married. This is because marriage is a temporary institution which anticipates and reflects the marriage of God and his people – the perfect marriage that God's people will enjoy after death in the new creation that God has prepared for them. This is why Jesus is described as the bridegroom and his people are portrayed as his bride (see Mark 2:19-20; Revelation 19:7-9).

Mark 13:14
What is "the abomination that causes desolation"?
A passage in another Gospel helps us to understand. Luke 21:20 substitutes the words "Jerusalem being surrounded by armies" for this phrase. It refers to the occasion in AD 65 when Roman armies surrounded Jerusalem after a political uprising. After a horrific five-year war, the Roman armies entered the city, desecrated the temple, and then proceeded to pull it down and destroy the city. Jesus' words here in Mark 13 came true.

Mark 13:32
Why does Jesus not know the date of his own return?
Some suggest that Jesus could not be perfect, or God, if he does not know this important fact. But for God the Son to enter the world as a human being, it meant that he "made himself nothing" (Philippians 2:7). For example, as a child, Jesus had to grow in wisdom, just as all children do. He wasn't born with complete knowledge built in. Mark 13:32 is one of those small details which actually point toward the honesty of biblical history. If someone were deliberately making up a story about Jesus being the Son of God, this verse seems a very counter-productive detail to include – unless of course, it was actually what Jesus said.

Mark 14:12
What are "the Festival of Unleavened Bread" and "the Passover lamb"?
God commanded the Israelites to keep the annual feasts of Passover and Unleavened Bread to remind themselves of how he had rescued them from slavery in Egypt (Exodus 12:14-20). Israel could only be saved from the tenth plague, the death of the firstborn, by killing a lamb, eating its roasted flesh with bitter herbs and unleavened bread, and smearing the blood on the door frames. Wherever there was blood on a door, the Lord "passed over" the house and spared the firstborn (Exodus 12:1-13). The meal eaten in Mark 14:12-26 takes place at Passover. Jesus' death would be the true means of rescue from God's judgment; it would be the true Passover. This is why Jesus is sometimes referred to as the Lamb of God.

Mark 14:24
What is the "blood of the covenant"?
Passover commemorates rescue from slavery in Egypt, and from the wrath of God, by the pouring out of blood (Exodus 12:23). That rescue was followed by a covenant (an agreement made by God on behalf of his people) that was sealed by a blood sacrifice (Exodus 24:6). This mirrors Jesus' sacrificial death. He bled and died to turn God's wrath away from us, and to start a new covenant.

Mark 15:33
Was the darkness an eclipse of the sun?
Not possible. Jesus was crucified at the time of the Jewish Passover, which is always at full moon. At full moon, it is impossible to have a solar eclipse. Physically there is no adequate explanation of the darkness, other than that it was a super-

natural sign at the time of mankind's darkest deed – killing the Son of God.

Mark 16:9-20

Why do we stop reading at Mark 16:8?
Most scholars agree that Mark's Gospel ends at chapter 16:8, with the women responding to Jesus' resurrection by running away terrified. The ending provokes a question in the reader: how will YOU respond to Jesus' life, death and resurrection?

Verses 9-20 of Mark chapter 16 seem to be attempts by later writers to add a fuller resurrection ending to Mark. However, as the NIV note makes clear, the oldest manuscripts do not include this section. The style and vocabulary are different from the rest of Mark. This doesn't mean that Mark 16:9-20 is untruthful; most of these details also appear in the other Gospels. It just means that they were probably not in Mark's original document.

QUESTIONS ABOUT
CHRISTIAN BELIEF

How do you know that God exists?

- Many philosophical and scientific arguments have been used over the years to show that believing in God is rational and sensible. But ultimately, even the best of these lead only to general belief in a God, not specifically to the God of the Bible. It is usually more helpful to talk about Jesus and his claim to be God.

- We can know God exists because he became a man: Jesus Christ. This is the core of Jesus' answer to Philip's question in John 14:8-9. It's worth looking this up and reading it together if the question arises.

- Jesus was a real person who lived in Palestine 2000 years ago – the historical evidence for this stacks up (see next question).

- Jesus claimed to be God (e.g. John 5:18; 20:28-29) and his actions bore out that claim. Check out his claims as you read through Mark and come to *Christianity Explored.*

Why should we believe what the Bible says?

- Try not to get involved in defending passages from all over the Bible. Instead, start with the reliability of the Gospels. See "Can We Rely On Mark's Gospel?" in this Leader's Handbook on p127. If we can rely on the Gospels, and what Jesus says in the Gospels about the trustworthiness of Scripture, then it makes sense to trust the Bible as a whole.

- Historical evidence in the New Testament is confirmed at a number of points by non-Christian historical writers – e.g. Tacitus and Josephus – and also by archaeological evidence.

- The New Testament documents were written soon after the events they describe.

- This New Testament documentation is extensive, coming from as many as ten authors, eight of whom wrote independently of each other.

- The documents are historical in character as well as theological. They contain many verifiable details of the time and culture in which they were written.

- Textual criticism shows that the text of these documents has come down to us intact from the era in which they were written.

- The writers were people who suffered and died for what they believed, and were also of very high moral standing. They believed in telling the truth. It is highly unlikely they would make up these stories, or even "imagine" them.

- The Gospels are very uncomplimentary about the disciples who assisted in writing them. For example, Peter helped Mark write his Gospel – and yet Peter is shown to be a coward (Mark 14:66-72). Given that Peter was a leader in the early church, why would he include something like this? Unless, of course, it was just the inconvenient truth.

- The gospel accounts are too detailed to be legends. They're packed full of tiny details that apparently serve no purpose, unless explained simply as eyewitness details. Modern novels sometimes have this level of detail, but they didn't exist until about 300 years ago; it's unprecedented in an ancient document. The author C. S. Lewis (once Professor of English Literature at both Oxford and Cambridge) said, "I have been reading poems, romances, vision literature, legends and myths all my life. I know what they are like. I know none of them are like this."

Don't all good people go to heaven?

- What is "good"? How good is "good enough"?

- Some of us are better than others, but no one meets God's standards (see Romans 3:23).

- We are not good, because our hearts are "sin factories" (Mark 7:21-22).

- People who think they're "good enough" for heaven don't realize that they've broken what Jesus calls the first and most important of all God's commands: "Love the Lord your God with all your heart and with all your soul and with all your mind and with all your strength" (Mark 12:28-30). Rather than loving God, we love other things more (see the story of the rich man meeting Jesus in Mark 10:17-22). We may be "good" relative to others, but we can't be good enough for heaven if we break God's most important command.

- The opposite is, in fact, true. "Good" people go to hell; bad people go to heaven. Those who think they are good, and rely on that, will be lost. Only those who know they are lost are able to receive forgiveness and eternal life from Christ.

Why would a good God send people to hell?

- God is utterly holy and good. His character is what decides right and wrong in the universe.

- God must judge everyone. He would not be a just God if he ignored wrongdoing or evil. He will judge fairly and well.

- We know that punishments ought to fit the crime. Someone who murders deserves a worse punishment than someone who runs a red light. Is it possible that the reason we think hell is unfair is because we don't realize how serious our sin is?

- Jesus is the most loving person who ever lived, but it is he who teaches most about the reality of hell. He does so because he knows it is real, and doesn't want us to suffer the inevitable consequences of our rebellion against God.

- God has judged his Son, Jesus, on the cross. As a result, he went through hell, so we don't have to. When he died on the cross, he was dying in our place. For those who turn to him, Jesus took the punishment we deserve, so we can know God and enjoy him forever.

- If we understood how holy God is, we would be asking the opposite question: how can God allow anyone into heaven?

If God forgives everything, does that mean I can do what I like?

- God offers us forgiveness so that we can know and enjoy him. Why would we want to "do what we like" if, by doing so, it keeps us from enjoying him to the full, and puts us in danger of judgment?

How can we be sure that there is life after death?

- The Bible teaches that everyone will be resurrected after death in order to face judgment (Hebrews 9:27). For those who know and love Christ, there is nothing to fear, because the One appointed as Judge (Acts 17:31) is also the One who gave his life for them.

- Who do you trust for accurate information about life beyond the grave? The person who has been there and come back. If Jesus has been raised from the dead, then those who trust in him will also be delivered from death. (See John 11:25. Also Mark 12:24-27 and the note on that passage in "Questions From Mark's Gospel" on page 118.)

What about other religions?

- Sincerity is not truth. People can be sincerely wrong.

- If the different religions contradict each other (which they do at several major points), they cannot all be right.

- The question really is: has God revealed himself, and if so, how? Jesus claimed to be the unique revelation of God. He claimed to be God in the flesh. Are his claims valid? If Jesus is God, then logically, other religions must be wrong.

- Jesus claims he is the only way (John 14:6).

- Religions can do many good things: provide comfort, help, social bonding, etc. But all of them – apart from Christianity – teach that we must DO something in order to "earn" our place in heaven.

- By contrast, Jesus claims that we can never "earn" our way to heaven by doing good things. He claims that the only way we can know and enjoy God forever is if we trust in what HE (Jesus) has done on our behalf, not in what WE have done.

What about those who have never heard about Jesus?

- We can trust God to be just; he will judge people according to their response to what they know.

- Everyone has received some revelation, even if only from the created world (see Romans 1:18-19).

- Those who have had more revealed to them will be held more responsible (Matthew 11:20-24).

- You have heard, so you must do something about it – and leave the others to God, who will treat them fairly.

Isn't faith just a psychological crutch?

- It is true that faith in Christ provides an enormous psychological crutch! It gives hope, meaning and joy, even in the face of suffering and death. It is one of life's greatest joys to know for certain that you are perfectly known and yet perfectly loved by the Creator of the universe.

- But that doesn't mean Christian faith is "wishful thinking", some sort of imaginary story created to make us feel better in the face of life's hardships.

- On the contrary, Christian faith is founded on historical events: the life, death and resurrection of Jesus. The truth of these events – and therefore the truth of Christianity – doesn't depend on whether or not we "need" them to be true.

Why does God allow suffering?

- Much suffering is a direct result of our own sinfulness (e.g. that caused by drunkenness, greed, lust, etc.).

- But some is not (see John 9:1-3).

- All suffering results from the fallen nature of our world (see Romans 8:18-25).

- God uses suffering to discipline and strengthen his children (see Hebrews 12:7-11; Romans 5:3-5).

- God also uses suffering to wake people up so that they understand that there is a judgment coming to our pain-filled world (Luke 13:1-5).

- Unlike many other "gods", the God of the Bible knows intimately what it is like to suffer. God the Son suffered loneliness, grief, temptation, alienation from loved ones, mockery, isolation, bereavement, hunger, thirst, homelessness, mental anguish and the worst physical agonies humans have been able to invent. As a result, he relates to and sympathizes with our deepest pain (Hebrews 4:15). He is not distant from it, or disinterested in it.

- But the God of the Bible does more than show mere sympathy; he has done something decisive to end all human suffering. Jesus suffered and died so that those who know and love him can one day enjoy a new creation, where there will be no suffering or pain of any kind.

- Though we don't know all the reasons why God allows suffering in every case, it seems reasonable to assume that our "not knowing" doesn't necessarily mean suffering must be pointless. At the time Jesus suffered and died, the disciples would have felt that his death was a horrible evil, a pointless tragedy. And yet, if the biblical claim is true, his suffering and death was the means by which countless millions of lives have been saved.

Hasn't science disproved Christianity?

- Start by asking what they mean by the question. They may have some specific point which needs addressing – and that will require some research. During the session, it's best to avoid having technical discussions about evolution, carbon dating, etc. as you're likely to run over time, or leave other members of the group bored or left out.

- Most people mean: "Hasn't the theory of (macro)evolution replaced the idea of creation, and so disproved Christianity?" People usually are not talking about archaeology which, incidentally, backs up the Bible at almost every point.

- Ask what conclusions they are drawing from evolution. Even if they believe it gives an account of how life on earth came to be so varied, it doesn't answer the question of how life came to be in the first place. How did something come from nothing – literally nothing, not even empty space. It also doesn't answer the question of WHY things exist: what is the purpose of life? What should we live FOR?

- Steer the conversation towards talking about God's existence (see above) and towards Jesus. If Jesus is God, it puts the creation/evolution debate in a completely different perspective.

If Jesus is God's Son, how can he be God too?

- Jesus lets himself be described as the "Son of God" – a term which can mean that he is the King of God's people, but can also be a claim that he is much more.

- Jesus acts in the New Testament in the way that God does in the Old Testament. He speaks as God speaks, and does things that only God can do (raises the dead, forgives sins, controls nature,

etc.). His words and actions show that he is making a claim to be God.

- Christians do not believe that there are many gods, and that Jesus is just one of them. The Bible teaches that God is a "tri-unity" or "Trinity": one God in three "Persons". The three Persons are Father, Son and Spirit, all of whom are fully God. For one example of this biblical teaching, see the description of Jesus' baptism in Mark 1:10-11, where God's tri-unity is clearly seen.

- This is complex and hard to grasp fully – but wouldn't it be strange if the nature of God himself were an easy thing for finite humans to understand?

Why does God hate sex?

- It would be strange if the Creator of sex hated it! He created sex to be beautiful, enjoyable and extremely powerful.

- Our Creator knows best what leads to our joy and health. He designed sex to be enjoyed by a husband and wife within the mutual protection of marriage (see Jesus' words in Matthew 19:4-5). Sex joins people together in a way that is more than physical.

- Marriage is a temporary institution which anticipates and reflects a far greater marriage: the marriage of God and his people, which God's people will enjoy in the new creation. This is why Jesus is described as the bridegroom and his people are portrayed as his bride (see Mark 2:19-20; Revelation 19:7-9).

- But those who, for whatever reason, remain single all their lives will not miss out on anything if their hope is in Christ. Not even the very best earthly marriage will come close to the experience of being fully known and loved in the new creation (Revelation 19:7-9).

Christians are hypocrites – so how can Christianity be true?

• The failure of many Christians to live according to their stated beliefs does not invalidate Jesus' claims to be God.

• The Bible says that Jesus alone is perfect, and it is honest about the failures and weakness of his followers. The disciples in Mark are constantly making mistakes.

• Jesus taught that there will always be false teachers and fakes (Mark 13:21-22) who pretend they are Christians but who are not. This is true today.

• Everyone is a hypocrite to some extent. How many of us fully and perfectly "practise what we preach"? But Jesus calls those who follow him to change and grow more like him.

Note: For answers to these and other questions, see *If You Could Ask God One Question* by Paul Williams and Barry Cooper. It's ideal for leaders and for group members. More technical but still very readable is *The Reason for God* by Tim Keller.

CAN WE RELY ON
MARK'S GOSPEL?

• *This material is a copy of the notes found on page 71 of the group member's Handbook.*

Who? When? Why?

Mark was a close friend and companion of Peter, who was one of Jesus' disciples. Peter was an "apostle" (one of those specifically called to witness the life, death and resurrection of Jesus). Peter wrote two letters to the first-century Christian churches. In one of them he said, "I will make every effort to see that after my departure (i.e. his death) you will always remember these things." (2 Peter 1:15). He was referring to the things he saw and knew about Jesus. He passed them on to others like Mark. Peter died in the mid 60s of the 1st century. The evidence suggests that Mark wrote his Gospel around that period.

No doubt Mark was influenced by Peter's desire for the news about Jesus to be told to others in later generations, so he wrote it down in a book. His opening sentence reveals the subject of his book: "The beginning of the gospel about Jesus Christ, the Son of God." (Mark 1:1).

Jesus died, rose again and returned to heaven around AD 30. Mark wrote about 30 years later – well within the lifetime of those who lived through the events he recorded. So Mark had to write accurately. Any inconsistencies between what people saw and what he wrote would have discredited him.

Has Mark's book changed over time?

How different is Mark's original book from the book that we have today?

We don't have Mark's original to compare with the book we call Mark's Gospel. This is normal for ancient documents, since the original copy would have been written on material such as papyrus or parchment, which would eventually rot away.

For this reason historians assess the reliability of copies of an original by asking the following questions:

• How old are the copies?

• How much time has elapsed between the writing of the original document and the production of the copies that now exist?

• How many copies have been found?

The table below answers these questions for three widely-trusted historical works, and compares them with the New Testament (including Mark's Gospel).

As the table shows, the oldest surviving copies of Mark were produced 240 years after his original (a comparatively short time) and an astonishing 14,000 copies exist today.

So we can have great confidence that what we read is what Mark wrote.

For more detail, *Can I Really Trust The Bible?* by Barry Cooper is a short, easy read.

	Date of original document	Date of oldest surviving copy	Approximate time between original and oldest surviving copy	Number of ancient copies in existence today
THUCYDIDES' HISTORY OF THE PELOPONNESIAN WAR	c. 431–400 BC	AD 900 plus a few late 1st-century fragments	1,300 years	73
CAESAR'S GALLIC WAR	c. 58–50 BC	AD 825	875 years	10
TACITUS' HISTORIES AND ANNALS	c. AD 98–108	c. AD 850	750 years	2
THE WHOLE NEW TESTAMENT (MARK'S GOSPEL)	AD 40–100 (AD 60–65)	AD 350 (3rd century)	310 years (240 years or less)	14,000 (approx 5,000 Greek; 8,000 Latin; 1,000 in other languages)

MAP OF PLACES IN
MARK'S GOSPEL

This map is included on page 75 of the group member's Handbook.

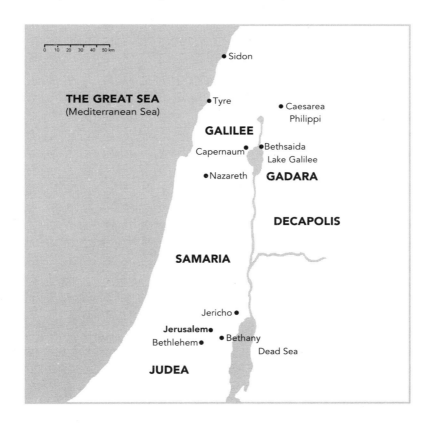

VIDEO SCRIPTS

Video Episode 1: Good news

What's the most beautiful sight you've ever seen?

For me it was probably Table Mountain in South Africa. I was visiting my twin sister, and some friends and I took a cable car to the top. I remember watching the sun break through the clouds and light up Cape Town 3000 feet below. It was so stunning we lost all track of our conversation and just stood there in silence.

What would it be for you?

And when you saw what you saw, I wonder if you asked yourself the same questions I did... what kind of power could have produced something so achingly beautiful that it reduces a human being to sheer, wordless wonder?

Did all this beauty really just happen by chance?

How did life begin, without life to create it in the first place?

And even if I do decide it all happened completely by chance, why is there anything here at all?

Why is there something...
and not nothing?

Then there are the stars... millions of millions of miles above us... Apparently, there are at least 100 billion stars in our galaxy alone, and scientists estimate there are at least 100 billion galaxies in the universe.

And it's not just the larger things in life that are truly remarkable... it's the smaller things too.

There are 75000 miles of blood vessels crammed inside us and at least 50 trillion cells. If the DNA from a single human cell were stretched out, it would measure about six feet in length.

So if all the DNA contained within the cells of a single human being was stretched out and laid end to end, it would reach all the way to the moon. And back again. Eight thousand times.

You're amazing, and if you saw something that stunning in a gallery, or heard something that beautiful on the radio, you'd instinctively ask, "Who created it?".

And if someone were to tell you that this incredible piece of art or music just came together by itself, without any author to create it, would you believe them?

The Bible quite unashamedly says that all this natural beauty is meant to point us towards God, the one who created the extraordinary scale and complexity of the universe we live in, and the bodies we inhabit.

But as a younger man I had a real problem with all that. Although my experience of the universe was that it really was extraordinary, Christianity definitely was not.

First of all, it was incredibly dull. I used to go to church about once a month, and when I did, I just sat there counting the number of bricks up the wall.

Secondly, I couldn't see what it had to do with me. I couldn't relate to the religious people I met, and I couldn't see the point of reading a book written 2000 years ago and 2000 miles away. I thought it was a bunch of rules telling me how to live my life, and actually, my life was pretty good so I didn't need any of them.

Then thirdly, and most importantly, I just thought it wasn't true. I didn't have a problem with Christmas, and as you can probably guess I had no problem with Christmas stuffing, but Christianity itself was make-believe. I never mistook it for the real world.

But then my brother did something that started to change the way I thought about Christianity. He opened a Bible and showed me the very first sentence of a book called Mark. It says this:

"The beginning of the gospel about Jesus Christ..." (Mark 1:1)

He said to me, "Rico, you just don't understand what Christianity's about. You think it's all about... churches... and rules... and leaving your brain at the door... and having all your fun spoiled.

"But," he said to me, "That's not what it's about. The first sentence of Mark says that Christianity is about Christ."

He explained that the word "Christ" isn't Jesus' second name. It's a title, like President or Prime Minister. And it means "God's only chosen King".

And "Christ" was an extremely dangerous word for Mark to use here, because at the time he was writing, Roman Emperors were said to have divine authority.

To speak of Jesus as God's only true representative on earth was the kind of thing that got you thrown into the Coliseum to be torn apart by wild animals.

Mark's claim that Jesus is the Christ, God's only chosen King, is just as controversial today. I wonder what you make of it?

Then my brother pointed me back to the first sentence in Mark...

"The beginning of the gospel about Jesus Christ..." (Mark 1:1)

He said, "Rico, not only is Christianity about Jesus Christ... it's the 'gospel' about Jesus Christ."

The word "gospel" literally means "good news", but that doesn't really do it justice. It's more like the announcement that war is finally over.

It's the kind of news that makes people dance in the streets and hug complete strangers, it's that good.

So one thing I'd like to say as we start to explore Mark together is this. When you hear what you're about to hear, if you don't think it's the best news you've ever heard, you can be absolutely certain you've not understood it.

And it would be so easy to miss. Have you ever had the experience of walking down the main street of a city, and being offered a leaflet? You ignore it, or take it and then ignore it, because you don't think it will do you any good.

Well, there was an experiment conducted by a London newspaper. They got a man to stand just here, outside Oxford Circus tube station, offering people a leaflet. On the leaflet was the free offer of five pounds. All you had to do was bring the leaflet back to the man and he would hand you the cash right there on the spot.

Hordes of people passed him. And in three hours only eleven people came back for the money. They thought they already knew what he was handing out; that it wouldn't do them any good. So they either didn't bother to take it, they didn't bother to read it, or if they did read it, they simply refused to believe it.

Please don't make the same mistake with Mark's Gospel. Make time to pick it up and read it. Take a look at what Mark has to say about Jesus, and as you do that I hope you'll begin to see why Mark describes Jesus as "good news".

No one knows exactly when Mark wrote his Gospel, but it was most likely between 45 and 60 AD, within about 20 years of Jesus' death. Mark was being guided by one of Jesus' closest followers, Peter – a man who was an actual eyewitness of the remarkable events that occurred.

And they were remarkable events. Right from the beginning of Mark's Gospel, strange things start to happen. Supernatural things.

"At that time Jesus came from Nazareth in Galilee and was baptised by John in the Jordan.

"As Jesus was coming up out of the water, he saw heaven being torn open and the Spirit descending on him like a dove. And a voice came from heaven:

"'You are my Son, whom I love; with you I am well pleased.'" (Mark 1:9-11)

Heaven gets torn open, the Holy Spirit comes down on Jesus, and God the Father announces, "You are my Son".

And if you're thinking to yourself, well this is just flat-out weird, you're not the only one. Mark tells us that people thought exactly the same thing 2000 years ago, including Jesus' closest followers.

But maybe they should have expected it. Early in Mark's Gospel we read a 700-year-old prediction that someone called "the Lord" was on his way.

In other words, get ready. God is coming to meet you.

The prediction also says that a messenger in the desert will tell people that the Lord is coming. That messenger, according to Mark chapter 1, was a man called John the Baptist.

Mark tells us that…

"The whole Judean countryside and all the people of Jerusalem went out to him." (Mark 1:5)

They flocked to him because, if God was coming, they knew they needed to be ready. They knew from their own experience they were not the people they wanted to be, let alone the people God wanted them to be.

So John offers them baptism with water, as a sign of being washed clean, of being forgiven. When the person was lowered into the water, it was a symbol of dying to the old self; and when they were lifted out of the water, it was a symbol of being raised to new life.

But John knows that when the Lord himself comes, he will offer them – and us – so much more.

"After me will come one more powerful than I, the thongs of whose sandals I am not worthy to stoop down and untie. I baptise you with water, but he will baptise you with the Holy Spirit." (Mark 1:7-8)

What John is saying is absolutely stunning. He's claiming that Jesus Christ will not only offer complete forgiveness to all those who put their trust in him. He will also fill those people with God's Holy Spirit, who will radically transform their lives.

To those who know they are not the people they want to be, let alone the people God wants them to be, this is the best, the most remarkable news in the world.

But is it true?

It's certainly true that what Mark reports isn't the kind of thing people normally experience. And if Jesus is just an ordinary man, then what we read here is simply not believable.

But if, as Mark claims, Jesus is much more than that, then it shouldn't surprise us that extraordinary things are starting to happen.

And that is the beginning of the good news that Mark has for us: God has actually revealed himself to us in human history through Jesus Christ. When we look at Jesus, all the guessing games about God stop.

The good news, according to Mark, is that Jesus really is the Christ, God's only chosen King.

But Mark is just getting started…

Video Episode 2: Identity

Not so long ago I was invited out to lunch, and as I'd arrived a bit early, I waited on the stairs just off the main dining room.

Standing opposite me was another man. I vaguely recognized him, but thought nothing of it, so – as English people do – we gave each other a sheepish nod… and stood there awkwardly for five minutes in total silence. This lasted from 12.55 until one o'clock.

Anyway, at one o'clock, a man came from around the corner, looked up at the man beside me and exclaimed, "Ah William, there you are, we're in the private dining room".

Turns out it was Prince William.

I'd been with him for five whole minutes, and we had nothing better to do than talk to each other, and I hadn't said a single word!

And now I'd lost the opportunity.

It could have been so different.

I'm not saying that those five minutes would have changed my life, and I don't suppose we'd have become lifelong friends or anything like that, but I know the conversation would have been memorable.

Sadly, all I saw was a handsome well-dressed 25-year-old with thinning blond hair. What I didn't see... was my future King. Now in William's case, missing his identity doesn't really matter. I just missed out on a once-in-a-lifetime conversation (and arguably so did he) but that's about it.

Sometimes, though, getting someone's identity right really does matter. Because if we don't get Jesus' identity right, we'll relate to him in totally the wrong way – or even ignore him completely.

And missing this King's identity would be disastrous.

That's why Mark gives us the historical evidence we need so that we can recognize Jesus for who he is – evidence that comes from the firsthand, eyewitness accounts of people who spent years by Jesus' side.

We're going to focus on five ways that Mark reveals Jesus' identity. Mark wants us to understand, by showing Jesus' power and authority, that Jesus really does have the right to be in charge: that he really is God's only chosen King.

Our first block of evidence is about Jesus' power and authority to teach. Mark gives an example of this in chapter 1, verses 21 to 22:

"They went to Capernaum, and when the Sabbath came, Jesus went into the synagogue and began to teach. The people were amazed at his teaching, because he taught them as one who had authority, not as the teachers of the law." (Mark 1:21-22)

You see, what set Jesus apart from the other teachers was the way that he taught.

The teachers of the law didn't come up with their own material. They relied on the great teachers of the past, and just gave their opinions on what others had said.

But Jesus was very different. He didn't need to stand on anyone else's authority. He claimed authority of his own, and you can see the effect that this had on people. We read that they were "amazed" at his words and asked each other, "What is this? A new teaching – and with authority!" (Mark 1:27)

This young man, with hardly any education to speak of, was suddenly providing brilliant answers to questions that baffled even the wisest of teachers.

So he could teach, but was Jesus able to live out what he taught?

I have to say this was the first thing I found so compelling about Jesus.

At 16 I started to keep a journal. I decided I was such a great guy that I owed it to the world to preserve the details of my life.

What I found as I looked at what I'd written was my own selfishness. There was such a contradiction between the way I presented myself in my journal, and the way I actually lived in reality.

But Jesus was no hypocrite. For example, he taught, *"Love your enemies and pray for those who persecute you."* Later, as he was being killed, he prayed for his executioners, *"Father, forgive them, they do not know what they are doing"*. Now that is practising what you preach.

But Jesus wasn't just a teacher. Our second block of evidence shows that Jesus has power and authority over sickness. One example of this comes in Mark chapter 1 verses 29 to 31:

"As soon as they left the synagogue, they went with James and John to the home of Simon and Andrew. Simon's mother-in-

law was in bed with a fever, and they told Jesus about her. So he went to her, took her hand and helped her up. The fever left her and she began to wait on them." (Mark 1:29-31)

Here we see Jesus demonstrating absolute authority over sickness. Just a touch of his hand and the fever is cured – and this is not an isolated incident either.

Three verses later, in verse 34, we read that Jesus cured whole crowds of sick people. Soon after that, a man with leprosy comes to him. It was a disease so terrible that no one even wanted to go near those who were suffering with it. Filled with compassion, Jesus reaches out his hand and touches the man, and his touch instantly cures him. Mark also tells us that Jesus cured people of spiritual suffering as well as physical suffering, releasing people from demonic oppression.

By verse 12 of chapter 2, everyone is amazed, saying, "We've never seen anything like this".

As you might expect, someone with that kind of power does not go unnoticed elsewhere. For example, Josephus, a historian of Jesus' time who was not a Christian, called Jesus a "doer of wonderful deeds". Although people disagreed about where it came from, no one – not even Jesus' enemies – doubted Jesus' power.

Then thirdly, and perhaps even more amazingly, we see that Jesus has power and authority over nature.

Jesus and his followers are in a boat on the lake of Galilee, and this is what happens in chapter 4 verses 37 to 39.

"A furious squall came up, and the waves broke over the boat, so that it was nearly swamped. Jesus was in the stern, sleeping on a cushion. The disciples woke him and said to him, 'Teacher, don't you care if we drown?'

"He got up, rebuked the wind and said to the waves, 'Quiet! Be still!' Then the wind died down and it was completely calm." (Mark 4:37-39)

Now the Greek word translated "furious squall" actually means "whirlwind". As the waves break over the boat, nearly swamping it, Jesus' followers (some of whom are hardened fishermen) are convinced they're about to die.

In their terror they wake Jesus. But Jesus simply gets up, says a few words and immediately everything is perfectly calm.

The disciples then ask each other a question we may be asking ourselves:

"Who is this? Even the wind and the waves obey him!" (Mark 4:41)

However, in the next chapter the disciples witness something even more astonishing. They witness Jesus' power and authority… over death. That's our fourth block of evidence about Jesus' identity, and it's in Mark chapter 5.

"When Jesus had again crossed over by boat to the other side of the lake, a large crowd gathered around him while he was by the lake. Then one of the synagogue rulers, named Jairus, came there. Seeing Jesus, he fell at his feet and pleaded earnestly with him, 'My little daughter is dying. Please come and put your hands on her so that she will be healed and live.'" (Mark 5:21-23)

Here we have a religious leader, a synagogue ruler named Jairus, in agony because he is powerless to help his young daughter who is dying.

Imagine the desperation and powerlessness you would feel if your own child was dying. That's the emotional intensity here.

Death wasn't an issue for me until I was 16. But then my godfather was killed suddenly when he lost his footing on a cliff path. And then I discovered for myself how painful death is, not least because it severs relationships with people we dearly love… and loving relationships are so hard to come by.

I remember coming across a bereavement card that said, "Those whom we have loved never really go away". But that's a lie. That's the whole problem – they do go away and we miss them terribly.

"Some men came from the house of Jairus, the synagogue ruler. 'Your daughter is dead,' they said. 'Why bother the teacher any more?'

"Ignoring what they said, Jesus told the synagogue ruler, 'Don't be afraid; just believe.'" (Mark 5:35-36)

Now what kind of a man is able to say to a grieving father, "Don't worry, just put your trust in me"? It's either the voice of a man who is spectacularly misguided, or the voice of one who is supremely confident of his own power.

You've got to be very sure of yourself to say that to a man who has just lost his daughter.

"He did not let anyone follow him except Peter, James and John the brother of James. When they came to the home of the synagogue ruler, Jesus saw a commotion, with people crying and wailing loudly.

He went in and said to them, 'Why all this commotion and wailing? The child is not dead but asleep.' But they laughed at him.

"After he put them all out, he took the child's father and mother and the disciples who were with him, and went in where the child was. He took her by the hand and said to her, 'Talitha koum!' (which means, 'Little girl, I say to you, get up!'). Immediately the girl stood up and walked around (she was twelve years old). At this they were completely astonished." (Mark 5:37-42)

Well, you would be, wouldn't you? Jesus tells them the girl isn't dead – she's just sleeping. Then he takes the hand of the corpse, says "Get up", and the father is reunited with the daughter he thought was lost to him forever.

The message is clear. It's as easy for Jesus to raise someone from the dead as it is for us to rouse someone from sleep.

Now, if this is a man who has power and authority over death, surely it would be madness to ignore him, to say, "I'm just not interested in this" or, "This is boring" or, "Well, that's fine for you to believe". One day, you and I are going to die. After the evidence we've just seen, the question we must ask ourselves is this: "Can I trust Jesus with my own death"?

But I have to say "Quiet, be still" and "Get up" are not the most outrageous things Jesus says in Mark. For that we have to go our final block of evidence, in chapter 2 verses 1 to 5:

"A few days later, when Jesus again entered Capernaum, the people heard that he had come home. So many gathered that there was no room left, not even outside the door, and he preached the word to them. Some men came, bringing to him

a paralytic, carried by four of them. Since they could not get him to Jesus because of the crowd, they made an opening in the roof above Jesus and, after digging through it, lowered the mat the paralyzed man was lying on. When Jesus saw their faith, he said to the paralytic, 'Son, your sins are forgiven.'" (Mark 2:1-5)

Now, those words really are extraordinary. Here's a man who presumably wants to be cured of his paralysis – and Jesus wants to cure him of his sin. Why would Jesus think sin was a more pressing issue than the man's paralysis? To understand that, we need to understand what the Bible means by the word sin.

A while back a national newspaper had an article on "The Seven Deadly Sins" and the writer said this: "In this day and age sin has lost its sting. A bit of sinning is much more likely to be seen as a spot of grown-up naughtiness. The kind of thing that sends a delicious shock through the system."

That's what many people think of sin these days: it's not very serious, it's a bit of fun on the side. But the Bible says that there's nothing nice about sin. Jesus always taught that sin is man's biggest problem. It's not paralysis, not global warming, not terrorism or ecological disaster or poverty, not lack of education or spiritual enlightenment – but sin.

Sin isn't just doing naughty things. It's not just lust or laziness or whatever. According to the Bible, sin is ignoring our Creator in the world he has made. As we know, ignoring other human beings is damaging enough – to us and to them. And living without reference to the One who made us and gives us each breath is even more damaging. Because when I insist on my independence from the One who made me, and sustains my life, it will

lead to death. Not just here, but eternal death, described in the Bible as hell.

So that's why Jesus homes in on the problem of this man's sin. And the claim that Jesus makes here is that he has the power and authority to forgive our sin. You can see how staggering this is if you look at the way the religious leaders react.

"Now some teachers of the law were sitting there, thinking to themselves, 'Why does this fellow talk like that? He's blaspheming! Who can forgive sins but God alone?'" (Mark 2:6-7)

Now, they don't mind the paralytic being called a sinner – they know everyone's a sinner. Their problem is with Jesus claiming to be able to forgive sin. If sin is ignoring God in the world he has made, then only God has the authority to forgive it. After all, if we do a person wrong, then only the wronged person has the right to forgive us. And in this case, the wronged party is God himself.

The question is, does Jesus really have the authority to forgive sin? Does he really have the right to identify himself with Almighty God? Or is Jesus blaspheming, as the religious leaders are quietly thinking to themselves? To answer that question, Jesus does something amazing.

"Immediately Jesus knew in his spirit that this was what they were thinking in their hearts, and he said to them, 'Why are you thinking these things? Which is easier: to say to the paralytic, "Your sins are forgiven," or to say, "Get up, take your mat and walk"? But that you may know that the Son of Man has authority on earth to forgive sins...' He said to the paralytic, 'I tell you, get up, take your mat and go home.' He got up, took his mat and walked out in full view of them all. This

amazed everyone and they praised God, saying, 'We have never seen anything like this!'" (Mark 2:8-12)

As if to illustrate his claim to have God's authority and power, Jesus immediately cures the man's paralysis with a few words. But the healing is not an end in itself; he doesn't do it with a flourish, as if performing magic tricks at a circus. No, he cures this man, and countless others, in order to reveal to us his true identity. He is quite obviously behaving with God's authority and God's power... and he expects us to draw the obvious conclusion.

Mark shows us time and again that Jesus not only claims to have the authority of God, he also displays the power of God as he teaches, heals the sick, calms the storm, raises the dead and forgives sin. He acts in God's world, with God's authority.

Of course, if Jesus is actually God's Son, then it really matters. It gets very personal. Do I recognize who he is?

Will I listen to him as my teacher? Can I acknowledge that he has complete control over the circumstances of my life... over sickness... over nature... and even over my own death?

Can I see that he is the only one with the power and the authority to forgive my sin... or to leave it unforgiven?

Will I recognize him now, while I have the chance? Or will I recognize him later, when it's too late?

Video Episode 3: Sin

When I started college in 1991, I joined the rugby club. It was quite competitive, so I was sent a strict summer training schedule – which I immediately put in the bin.

Anyway, September rolled around and I arrived for club testing and training feeling fairly confident.

When I arrived, all the guys were very quiet – which was unusual.

Then suddenly the coach came in and said, "Right, we'll start with the bleep test".

The bleep test is a test where you run back and forth over twenty yards in time with a bleep that gets faster and faster. You run until you drop. In my case that was not long in coming.

I was the second to drop out, having collapsed and been physically sick.

Next we had to strip down to our shorts for the so-called "fat test".

(Why not leave this part of the story to the imagination?)

Basically, the fat test is when your fat content is measured by this contraption that pinches the flesh all over your body. As it turned out, there was actually one other person who had an even higher percentage of body fat than me. We became firm friends. Well, flabby friends really.

The results of all these tests were recorded and publicly announced. And it was extremely humiliating. Eventually, when all the tests had been completed, the coach got us all together and said, "Well, it's not comfortable, but at least we found out the truth on the training ground before the real questions get asked during a proper game".

Sometimes we experience things in life that give us a shocking dose of reality.

Things that expose us in an extremely uncomfortable way. But as our coach said, "It's better to find out the truth about ourselves while we still have time to do something about it".

We've already explored who Jesus is. The question now is, why did Jesus come?

Did he want to bring peace on earth? Was it to heal disease and end the sufferings of the world? Did he want to transform society, and give us an example of how we ought to live?

According to Mark, although there's an element of truth in all those options, they're not the main reason Jesus came.

When we look at the world, there's so much to marvel at. But who can honestly say the world is all good?

Estimates vary, but histories of the twentieth century suggest that at least 100 million people died violently in those hundred years – that is 2400 violent deaths every day.

The question is, why is the world like this? Jesus tells us the uncomfortable truth in Mark's Gospel. He insists that the reason there is something wrong with the world... is because there's something wrong with us.

Imagine for a moment a huge public gallery. On display for the whole world to see is the story of your life. It's a complete and truthful account, not only of everything you've ever said and done, but also of every thought that has ever crossed your mind.

Nothing is edited out. Everything is here, for everyone to look at.

Now I'm sure there'd be lots that you'd be relatively proud of: loving relationships,

real achievements, acts of kindness, moments of generosity, perhaps a flourishing career...

But there would also be thousands of things you'd want to keep out of the public eye.

Which bit of the wall would you most want to cover up? Maybe it's something nobody knows, not even your closest friend.

And it's not just the things we've said, done and thought that are a problem. There are the things we should have done and the words we should have said.

If my life were on those walls it would be a nightmare. I'd hate my life to be on display for everyone to see – I'd be so ashamed. I wouldn't be able to look people in the eye.

Could you, if you're being honest?

So what is the problem? Why is there so much to be ashamed of? Jesus gives us the answer in Mark chapter 7:

"What comes out of a man is what makes him 'unclean'. For from within, out of men's hearts, come evil thoughts, sexual immorality, theft, murder, adultery, greed, malice, deceit, lewdness, envy, slander, arrogance and folly. All these evils come from inside and make a man 'unclean'." (Mark 7:20-23)

So when we look at the world and see all the things that are wrong with it, we instinctively want to point the finger at others. But Jesus says the problem is much closer to home. The reason the world is not the way it's supposed to be is because we're not the way we're supposed to be.

And if we were to trace all the evil in the world back to its source, says Jesus, the place we'd end up is the human heart.

For the people of Jesus' day, the heart was not simply the pump that sends blood around the body, it was thought of as the seat of human personality. It was "the real you".

Why is it so hard to keep good relationships going? Why do we hurt those we love most? Why can't we automatically do what we know is the right thing? And why are we so often tempted to do what we know is wrong? Because each of us has a heart problem.

Unfortunately, according to Jesus, our problems don't end there. It's not just that we often treat each other and our world in a shameful way – we treat God in that way too.

In Mark chapter 12, Jesus tells us how we should relate to God:

"*Love the Lord your God with all your heart and with all your soul and with all your mind and with all your strength.*" (Mark 12:30)

Jesus calls this "the most important commandment", and with good reason. Because God made us, and sustains us, and gives us every good thing we enjoy, what should be our response to him? Jesus tells us. We should love God with all our heart, soul, mind and strength. And the really scary word here is "all". It means that no part of our lives is to be withheld from God. He is to have all of everything.

But that's not our heartbeat.

We decide exactly what we'll do with our heart, soul, mind and strength. We give our hearts to lots of things, but not to our Creator. We barely know his commands, let alone seek to obey them. We develop relationships with others, but neglect the very relationship for which we were primar-ily designed. And instead of loving God, we live as if we were God – and that's what the Bible calls sin.

So why did Jesus come?

According to Mark's Gospel, Jesus came to cure our heart problem: the problem of our sin. Here's what happens in Mark chapter 2 verses 15 to 17.

"*While Jesus was having dinner at Levi's house, many tax collectors and 'sinners' were eating with him and his disciples, for there were many who followed him. When the teachers of the law who were Pharisees saw him eating with the 'sinners' and tax collectors, they asked his disciples: 'Why does he eat with tax collectors and "sinners"?'*

"*On hearing this, Jesus said to them, 'It is not the healthy who need a doctor, but the sick. I have not come to call the righteous, but sinners.'*" (Mark 2:15-17)

Notice how uptight these people are with Jesus. They're called the Pharisees and teachers of the law, and they were the religious establishment. They were always at the synagogue, always praying, always trying to do the right thing, and they are furious here because Jesus is spending time with all the people they love to look down on – especially tax collectors, who were hated because they worked for the occupying Roman forces.

But the shock for us, as it was for many re-ligious people at the time, is Jesus' state-ment in verse 17. "*It is not the healthy who need a doctor, but the sick. I have not come to call the righteous, but sinners.*"

You see, Jesus knows that when we look at our world and the state of our hearts, no one can seriously claim to be righteous.

No one has managed to love God with all their heart, all their soul, all their mind and all their strength. If we were able to live like that, there'd be no reason for him to have come at all.

"No," says Jesus, "I haven't come to call people who think they're good, who think they've nothing to be ashamed of. I've come for people who can see what is going on in their own hearts. People who realize that they are desperately in need of a cure."

If that's you, then I hope you can begin to see why Mark describes Jesus as "good news".

The qualification for coming to Jesus is not "are you good enough?" It's "are you bad enough?" He's come for people who realize they're bad – not for people who think they're good. That's the real reason Jesus came.

And isn't it ironic that these religious people who think that their hearts are perfectly acceptable to God are the very ones who end up plotting to kill Jesus?

So Jesus says, "I have not come to call the righteous, but sinners". But why did Jesus feel the need to call sinners at all? For the answer to that question, we need to look at the most disturbing verses in Mark's Gospel, chapter 9 verses 43 to 48.

It's here that Jesus tells us just how serious our heart problem really is.

"If your hand causes you to sin, cut it off. It is better for you to enter life maimed than with two hands to go into hell, where the fire never goes out. And if your foot causes you to sin, cut it off. It is better for you to enter life crippled than to have two feet and be thrown into hell. And if your eye causes you to sin, pluck it out. It is better

for you to enter the kingdom of God with one eye than to have two eyes and be thrown into hell, where 'their worm does not die, and the fire is not quenched.'" (Mark 9:43-48)

I was in Australia, visiting a friend, and he took me to a beach on Botany Bay. So I decided I had to go for a swim. I was taking my shirt off when he said, "What are you doing?" I said, "I'm going for a swim". He said, "But what about those signs?"

I said, "Oh don't be ridiculous, I'll be fine". He said, "Listen mate, 200 Australians have been killed by sharks. You've got to decide whether those signs are there to save you or to ruin your fun. You're of age, you decide." And with that he walked off down the beach.

When we hear Jesus' words about hell, we have to ask ourselves, "Why would he talk like this?" Is he trying to manipulate us? Trying to scare us just so he can gain control of us?

Or is he giving us a loving warning?

For me, as I look at Jesus' life and the way he treated people, I see the most loving man who ever lived. Even people who were rejected by the rest of the world were deeply loved by him.

The reason Jesus warns us about hell is surely because he loves us and does not want us to go there. He knows that if we reject God throughout our lives, then ultimately God will be right to reject us. He knows that our sin, if left undealt with, will take us to a place of unimaginable and unending suffering. He warns us because he loves us.

But here's the problem. Jesus is not giving us the cure for our sin when he talks about cutting off a hand or a foot, or gouging out an eye. Even if we were to do that, the knife would never go deep enough.

It would never get to the heart of the human problem – which is the problem of the human heart.

The urgent reality is that our hearts are desperately in need of a cure, and no matter what we do, as history has shown, we cannot cure it ourselves. But that is why Jesus came.

As much as I hated the fat test and the bleep test, it was far better for me to be exposed as unfit on the training ground, than in front of spectators in a crucial game.

In the same way, Jesus exposes what we're really like, so that we can respond to him while there's still time.

We'll never understand why Jesus came until we see the reality of our own hearts. And if we don't see that, we'll go through life without noticing that actually… we are in terrible danger.

Video Episode 4: The cross

Sometimes there is a world of difference between the way things seem to be and the way things really are.

Twenty minutes before midnight on Sunday 14th April 1912, passengers on the upper decks of the Titanic felt three small bumps as the ship collided with an iceberg.

But most people thought nothing of it. In fact, some picked up ice that had fallen onto the deck, and started playing snowballs.

Below deck, however, things were very different. The ship's hull had buckled in several places. Rivets started to pop out below the waterline. Suddenly, Titanic was laid wide open to the Atlantic Ocean. Within three hours, the ship that was thought to be "unsinkable" had been completely swallowed up by the sea – together with 1589 passengers.

The question is, what do we see as we look at ourselves?

Do we only see the upper deck, the way we seem on the surface? Or are we able to see the way things really are, deep down?

You may have wondered why the cross is the symbol of Christianity. Why on earth would followers of Christ want to remind themselves of his death – especially a death that was so gruesome and agonizing?

But there's another way of seeing Jesus' death. Not as a tragic waste of life. But as a rescue.

If the problem deep down in our hearts is as serious as Jesus claims, then the cross suddenly becomes incredibly precious. Because those two pieces of wood are the only lifeboat we have.

Unlike most of the deaths we read about in biographies, Jesus went to his death willingly, and quite deliberately. In fact, he came to be killed, and he knew it. Here's what Mark says about Jesus in chapter 8 verse 31, and note that the phrase "Son of Man" is Jesus' way of referring to himself.

"He then began to teach them that the Son of Man must suffer many things and be rejected by the elders, chief priests and teachers of the law, and that he must be killed and after three days rise again." (Mark 8:31)

So Jesus taught his followers that he must be killed. And he tells us why in Mark chapter 10 verse 45:

"The Son of Man did not come to be served, but to serve, and to give his life as a ransom for many." (Mark 10:45)

To understand exactly what that means, we need to read an account of Jesus' death.

"They brought Jesus to the place called Golgotha (which means The Place of the Skull). Then they offered him wine mixed with myrrh, but he did not take it. And they crucified him. Dividing up his clothes, they cast lots to see what each would get.

"It was the third hour when they crucified him. The written notice of the charge against him read: THE KING OF THE JEWS. They crucified two robbers with him, one on his right and one on his left. Those who passed by hurled insults at him, shaking their heads and saying, 'So! You who are going to destroy the temple and build it in three days, come down from the cross and save yourself.'

"In the same way the chief priests and the teachers of the law mocked him among themselves. 'He saved others,' they said, 'but he can't save himself! Let this Christ, this King of Israel, come down now from the cross, that we may see and believe.' Those crucified with him also heaped insults on him.

"At the sixth hour darkness came over the whole land until the ninth hour.

"And at the ninth hour Jesus cried out in a loud voice, 'Eloi, Eloi, lama sabachthani?' – which means, 'My God, my God, why have you forsaken me?'

"When some of those standing near heard this, they said, 'Listen, he's calling Elijah.'

"One man ran, filled a sponge with wine vinegar, put it on a stick, and offered it to Jesus to drink. 'Now leave him alone. Let's see if Elijah comes to take him down,' he said.

"With a loud cry, Jesus breathed his last.

"The curtain of the temple was torn in two from top to bottom. And when the centurion, who stood there in front of Jesus, heard his cry and saw how he died, he said, 'Surely this man was the Son of God!'" (Mark 15:22-39)

"At the sixth hour, darkness came over the whole land until the ninth hour." Now Mark is counting according to the Jewish system of time keeping, so the sixth hour would have been the middle of the day. At the very moment when the sun should have been at its brightest, darkness fell.

All this takes place during the Jewish festival of Passover, a festival that was always held during a full moon. So the darkness Mark tells us about cannot be a solar eclipse. Something else is happening here.

Time and again in the Bible, light symbolizes God's favour, while darkness represents God's anger and judgment. Something supernatural is occurring at the cross, and the clear message is that God is angry.

Now we won't understand this if we see God's anger as something that is unpredictable and wild, the product of a quick temper. Some of us have seen that kind of anger in ourselves, in friends and close relatives, and we know how ugly it is.

But God's anger is not like that. It is his settled, controlled, personal hostility to all that is wrong. Wrongdoing matters to God, whether we ourselves have done it to others, or if it has been done to us – and some of us have been treated terribly in our lives. God cares about that. Because he is a God of love, and a God of justice, he cannot simply ignore wrongdoing as if it did not matter. After all, we care about the wrongdoing we see in the world. Can we expect our loving Creator to care any less?

So as Jesus was dying on the cross, darkness came over the whole land. God was acting in anger to punish sin. Listen to Jesus' words in chapter 15 verse 34:

"At the ninth hour Jesus cried out in a loud voice 'Eloi, Eloi lama sabachthani?' - which means, 'My God, my God, why have you forsaken me?'" (Mark 15:34)

On the cross, Jesus was in some way "forsaken" or abandoned by God, as God punished sin.

But Jesus had led a completely sinless life. Not even his fiercest enemies could find any fault with him. So why would God be punishing him? And why is Jesus allowing himself to go through this?

Remember that Jesus said he came "to give his life as a ransom for many" (Mark 10:45).

The remarkable truth is that Jesus is giving himself up to be punished on our behalf. He is bearing the punishment that our sin deserves, so that we can be rescued.

It's not as if God the Son is some innocent third party being picked on by God the Father. As the Bible says elsewhere, "God was pleased to have all his fullness dwell in Jesus". In other words, Jesus was fully God.

As we look at the cross, we see God rescuing us by sacrificing himself.

Remember the public gallery containing the record of your life. All of your thoughts, words and actions are up on the walls for everyone to see. There's lots there that we would feel reasonably proud of, but if we're honest, there are other things that we'd want to remain hidden – perhaps especially in our thought life.

Sir Arthur Conan Doyle, the creator of Sherlock Holmes, once sent a message to the twelve most respectable people he knew, to see how they'd respond. The message simply said: "Flee, all is revealed!" Within 24 hours, six of these "respectable people" had left the country.

We all have secrets that we would hate to have exposed, but the Bible tells us that all of it has been recorded. Not just the way we've treated others, but the way we've treated God as well.

And all of this separates us from God.

But because Jesus took our sin upon himself, he suddenly experienced a terrible sense of being in some way separated from his Father. That's why Jesus cried out, "My God, my God, why have you forsaken me?" as he hung on the cross.

Jesus was taking upon himself all the punishment that our sin, everything on this film, deserves.

It's a stunning truth. He died as my substitute. In my place. Taking the punishment I deserve.

The result of Jesus' extraordinary self-sacrifice is this: Jesus paid the price for our sin, so that we never have to. The amazing reality is that Jesus loved me enough to die for my sin – for my sin, and for the sin of everyone who puts their trust in him.

It's as if the film has been wiped completely clean.

And if we want a demonstration that our sin really has been paid for, that Jesus' rescue really was successful, remember what Mark tells us in verses 37 and 38.

"With a loud cry, Jesus breathed his last.

"The curtain of the temple was torn in two from top to bottom." (Mark 15:37-38)

With those words, Mark records the exact moment of Jesus' death, but then turns his attention to something that happens simultaneously in the temple, which is on the other side of the city. He wants us to understand that the two events are connected in some way.

When Jesus dies, the 30 foot high curtain in the temple, which was as thick as the span of a man's hand, was torn from top to bottom.

The thick curtain used to hang in the temple, dividing the people from the place where God was said to live. The curtain was like a big "no entry" sign. It said loudly and clearly that it's impossible for sinful people like you and me to walk into God's presence. Then suddenly, as Jesus dies on the cross, the curtain is ripped in two, by God, from top to bottom. It's as if God is saying, "Because of the cross, the way is now open for people to approach me. Their sin has been finally and fully paid for."

Mark's description of Jesus' death also focuses on the reactions of people who witness it. I wonder who you most identify with?

One group of people is the soldiers. It's their job to carry out the execution. This is how they react to the cross:

"Dividing up his clothes, they cast lots to see what each would get." (Mark 15:24)

For these soldiers, the main legacy of the cross is Jesus' clothes. They are absorbed in doing their job, and they do it very well. But in doing that, and in their desire for material things, they miss what is going on right in front of their eyes.

Many of us go through life doing our duty, working hard, paying the bills. The day-to-day busyness of our intense lives blinds us to the true significance of the cross.

Another group of people to witness the crucifixion are the religious leaders. Mark tells us that they mock Jesus among themselves.

"He saved others ... but he can't save himself! Let this Christ, this King of Israel, come down now from the cross that we may see and believe." (Mark 15:31-32)

These religious leaders are convinced that they already know the way to God, and the cross is not a part of that route. To them, the cross is nothing but a demonstration of weakness. They don't see that if Jesus were to come down from the cross, their sin could never be paid for.

It is often those of us who think of ourselves as "spiritual" or religious who are the most vicious enemies of the cross. Because we consider ourselves to be righteous and moral people, we will only deal with our sin on our own terms.

And then there's Pontius Pilate, the Roman Governor. He has a sign fixed to the cross. It reads: "THE KING OF THE JEWS". Mark makes it clear that Pilate knows Jesus is innocent. He offers to release Jesus, but the crowd want a man called Barabbas released instead. Time and again Pilate sticks up for Jesus. But in the end, he hands Jesus over to be crucified. So why does Pilate hand over an innocent man to be killed?

"Wanting to satisfy the crowd, Pilate released Barabbas to them. He had Jesus flogged, and handed him over to be crucified." (Mark 15:15)

Pilate is a crowd-pleaser. Although he knows that Jesus is innocent, the sound of the crowd causes him to lose his nerve, and he gives in to the evil desires of others. When he faces a world that despises Jesus, his good intentions are overcome by his own cowardice.

That's something most of us suffer from. Our longing for the approval of others makes us behave in ways that we know are wrong. What will people think of me if I were to start trusting Jesus?

By showing us these different reactions, it's as if Mark is saying, "OK, this is how others responded to what happened. What about you? What do you see as you look at the cross?"

Are we too busy like the soldiers? Too self-righteous like the religious leaders? Or too cowardly like Pilate?

But we've missed someone important.

Because Mark also records the reaction of a Roman centurion, a hard-bitten soldier who was a high-ranking military officer. This is how Mark describes it.

"And when the centurion, who stood there in front of Jesus, heard his cry and saw how he died, he said, 'Surely this man was the Son of God!'" (Mark 15:39)

This man had doubtless fought many campaigns and seen many men die, but he'd never seen a man die like this.

So our final possibility as we look at what happened at the cross is to do what the centurion did: we can recognize that Jesus is telling the truth. That he is indeed the Son of God.

Right at the heart of London is the Old Bailey, the home of British justice. At the top is the golden statue of Lady Justice. She holds the scales of justice in one hand and the sword of judgment in the other. The message is clear: if we are found to be guilty, then the sword of judgment must fall.

But just across the London skyline from the Old Bailey, on top of St. Paul's Cathedral, is another golden symbol. It's a cross. And it's a powerful reminder that although the sword of God's judgment must fall, it fell on Jesus Christ.

So what will you do with your sin? Will you take it with you to the grave and to the judgment that must fall? Or will you let Jesus take it to the cross, and be rescued?

According to some reports, the orchestra on the deck of the Titanic played a hymn as the ship was sinking. The first line of that hymn speaks of rescue, not from the icy water of the Atlantic, but from a greater enemy. A rescue from sin and death. A rescue that removes the separation between sinful people and the loving God who made them. A rescue that is only possible through the death of God's only Son.

The words of the old hymn go like this:

"Nearer, my God, to thee, nearer to thee. Even though it be a cross that raises me."

Video Episode 5: Resurrection

Being reunited with those you love is one of the happiest experiences on earth. The familiar face, the reassuring voice, the comforting embrace. But imagine what it would be like to be reunited with someone you thought you'd lost forever. Not just someone who had changed jobs or moved away, but someone you thought you would never see again, never could see again.

When we think of those friends and family we've lost, it's devastating to think that they've gone. However hard we try, no medical or industrial advance can stop death from winning. Bodies, like these buildings, fall into disrepair and eventually fall apart.

Only one man in history has demonstrated absolute power and authority over death. He knew beforehand exactly how and when his own death would happen. And even more remarkably, he repeatedly claimed that he would be raised to life on the third day after his death:

"He then began to teach them that the Son of Man must suffer many things and be rejected by the elders, chief priests and teachers of the law, and that he must be killed and after three days rise again." (Mark 8:31)

"He said to them, 'The Son of Man is going to be betrayed into the hands of men. They will kill him, and after three days he will rise.'" (Mark 9:31)

"Again he took the Twelve aside and told them what was going to happen to him. 'We are going up to Jerusalem,' he said, 'and the Son of Man will be betrayed to the chief priests and teachers of the law. They will condemn him to death and will hand him over to the Gentiles, who will mock him and spit on him, flog him and kill him. Three days later he will rise.'" (Mark 10:32-34)

So much hangs on this. Because if Jesus was right, in advance, about his own resurrection from death, then it means he's trustworthy. He's not a liar and he's not a lunatic. It proves that we can trust him.

It also proves that there is genuine hope in the face of death. If Jesus really was raised from death, then we can be too.

But if Jesus was wrong about this, then Christianity is founded on a lie.

So how can we be sure about Jesus' staggering claim? First of all, we need to know that Jesus really did die.

At the end of his account of Jesus' death, Mark focuses on three women who have watched him suffer and die.

Not only have they watched him die, but two of them also watch him being buried. Mark tells us:

"Mary Magdalene and Mary the mother of Joses saw where he was laid." (Mark 15:47)

There's clearly no doubt in their minds that the only fit place for Jesus at this point is a tomb. Later, we read that they "bought spices so that they might go to anoint Jesus' body" (Mark 16:1).

These spices were used to embalm the dead. You wouldn't buy spices like that unless you were expecting to find a corpse.

But it wasn't only the women who were sure of Jesus' death.

"As evening approached, Joseph of Arimathea, a prominent member of the

Council, who was himself waiting for the kingdom of God, went boldly to Pilate and asked for Jesus' body. Pilate was surprised to hear that he was already dead. Summoning the centurion, he asked him if Jesus had already died. When he learned from the centurion that it was so, he gave the body to Joseph." (Mark 15:42-45)

It was unusual for crucifixion to result in death so quickly, so the Roman governor Pontius Pilate questions the centurion. The centurion confirms that, yes, Jesus was already dead.

Now, the Romans had many talents, but when it came to killing people, they were experts. If a centurion said someone was dead, he really was dead. Satisfied with the centurion's words, Pilate gives Joseph permission to remove the body from the cross.

"So Joseph bought some linen cloth, took down the body, wrapped it in the linen, and placed it in a tomb cut out of rock. Then he rolled a stone against the entrance of the tomb." (Mark 15:46)

As Joseph personally takes down the body from the cross, wraps it in linen, then places it in a tomb that was closed with a huge, heavy stone, he sees and feels nothing to suggest that the body was anything other than a corpse.

The evidence unanimously points to the fact that Jesus was dead. The disciples believed they would never again see Jesus alive.

In other words, Pontius Pilate, the centurion, Joseph of Arimathea and the women were all absolutely certain that Jesus had died.

The evidence unanimously points to the fact that Jesus was dead. The disciples would never see Jesus again.

But Mark's Gospel doesn't end there. He records what happens 36 hours after Jesus' death, very early on Sunday morning.

"When the Sabbath was over, Mary Magdalene, Mary the mother of James, and Salome bought spices so that they might go to anoint Jesus' body. Very early on the first day of the week, just after sunrise, they were on their way to the tomb and they asked each other, 'Who will roll the stone away from the entrance of the tomb?'" (Mark 16:1-3)

Once the Jewish holy day is over, the women return to the tomb where they'd seen the body being buried just 36 hours earlier. But they're about to get two major shocks.

"But when they looked up, they saw that the stone, which was very large, had been rolled away. As they entered the tomb, they saw a young man dressed in a white robe sitting on the right side, and they were alarmed." (Mark 16:4-5)

The first shock is when they see that the huge, heavy stone covering the entrance to the tomb has been rolled away.

Then comes the second shock as they go inside the tomb.

Jesus is nowhere to be seen. Instead, they see a young man dressed in a white robe. He tells them the reason Jesus is not there.

"'Don't be alarmed,' he said. 'You are looking for Jesus the Nazarene, who was crucified. He has risen!

"'He is not here. See the place where they laid him. But go, tell his disciples and Peter, "He is going ahead of you into Galilee. There you will see him, just as he told you."'" (Mark 16:6-7)

The one they thought was lost to them forever, the one they thought they would never see again, was waiting for them in Galilee. The place they had first met him – where everything started.

Other biblical accounts tell us there were at least ten separate occasions when Jesus appeared to his disciples after his death. We also read that more than 500 people saw him at the same time.

And this was no ghost or hallucination.

He had a physical body that could eat and drink, that could be talked to and touched. As the years passed, many of the disciples ended up joyfully dying for their faith, simply because they knew beyond any doubt that Jesus was indeed raised from death. They had seen it with their own eyes, and no threat or torture could make them deny what they knew was true.

They had seen, firsthand, that Jesus had triumphed over death, so death no longer had any fear for them or any power over them.

But Mark is under no illusions about the outrageousness of this claim. He doesn't gloss over the struggle to believe what has just happened. In fact, he says this:

"Trembling and bewildered, the women went out and fled from the tomb. They said nothing to anyone, because they were afraid." (Mark 16:8)

Even though Jesus had told them repeatedly in advance that it was all part of the plan, it's still too much for them to fully understand or accept.

And it may be that it's a struggle for you too. The temptation may be to forget all the evidence we've seen about who Jesus

is, and what he said he would do. Like the women, our instinct may be to run away from the resurrection, and say nothing to anyone.

But just as death was not the end for Jesus, so it won't be the end for us. Remember the words of the young man in the tomb. He told the women to tell the disciples:

"He is going ahead of you into Galilee. There you will see him, just as he told you." (Mark 16:7)

You see, it is not only the disciples who will see the risen Jesus. You will see him too. Acts 17 verse 31 tells us:

"For God has set a day when he will judge the world with justice by the man he has appointed. He has given proof of this to all men by raising him from the dead." (Acts 17:31)

In other words, there will be a day of judgment for all of us. The resurrection guarantees that, one day, we will all be raised physically from the dead. And Jesus will be our judge on that day. The only question is, are we ready to meet him?

One man who certainly was not ready was Peter, the fisherman from Galilee who had been one of Jesus' closest disciples. The one who guided Mark as he wrote his book. Peter was the disciple who had earlier criticized Jesus for predicting his own death and resurrection. Who had fallen asleep when Jesus had told him to keep watch. Who had told Jesus, "Even if I have to die with you, I will never disown you", and then, that same night, had denied even knowing Jesus. Not once, but three times.

We know that Peter felt the terrible weight of his own sin. Mark tells us that as soon as he disowned Jesus for the third time…

"...Peter remembered the word Jesus had spoken to him: 'Before the rooster crows twice you will disown me three times.' And he broke down and wept." (Mark 14:72)

Peter wept because he knew his sin had finally caught up with him. And there was nothing he could do to put it right.

But remember the words spoken by the man in the empty tomb, after Jesus is raised:

"Go, tell his disciples and Peter, 'He is going ahead of you into Galilee. There you will see him, just as he told you.'" (Mark 16:7)

It's a beautiful detail.

Having died to pay for sin, and having risen from death to prove that sin was truly paid for, Jesus wants Peter to know that he is included. If he would only trust Jesus, then all of his sin – every denial, every failure to love God as he should – would be fully and finally forgiven. The friends would be reunited.

One of the first funerals I ever took was for a professional musician called Stuart Spencer, who died of leukaemia in his late thirties. I saw him three days before he died, and I'll always remember my last visit to him. I was feeling emotional and without thinking I just said, "Stuart, what's it like to die?"

And I'll never forget his answer. He looked at me very calmly and said, "Rico, Christ has risen. The resurrection may be precious to you, but I'm going to stand before God in a few days' time. Do you have any idea how precious it is to me?"

You see, Stuart knew he was a sinner, just like Peter, just like you and me.

But he also knew for certain that Christ had died and risen for sinners. And because of that, he knew what awaited him beyond death: a real, physical resurrection of his body, a body that will eat and drink, be talked to and touched. A body that will never again see sorrow or suffering, disease or decay.

He also knew who awaited him, ready to welcome him. The familiar face, the reassuring voice, the comforting embrace.

Because of the certainty of the resurrection, Stuart could joyfully and calmly trust Jesus with his own death.

Can you?

Video Episode 6: Grace

Dad: You can open your eyes now.

[Girl opens gift.]

Mum: So? What do you think?

Girl: How much do I owe you?

If God were to say to you, "Why should I give you eternal life?", what would you say?

[Series of images of people on screen holding cards saying things like, "I'm a good person", "I don't steal", etc]

... And that's why you should give me eternal life.

The man we read about in Mark chapter 10 is very much like that. He's what you might call "a good person".

Two other writers in the Bible tell us about the same event, and together with Mark they help us build up a picture of what this man was like. Matthew tells us the man was young, Luke adds the detail that he was a "ruler" of some kind. And it's clear from Mark that he was rich, morally upright, spiritually-minded, and very religious.

So he has everything going for him: he's young, he's rich and he's powerful. And those who know him think of him as a good man: he would have been very well respected. He's exactly the sort of person many of us would like to be.

But there's also a vulnerability about him: he runs up to Jesus and falls on his knees – which in my experience is typically not something rich people do – and asks Jesus a question.

And it's the most important question anyone could ask.

"As Jesus started on his way, a man ran up to him and fell on his knees before him. 'Good teacher,' he asked, 'what must I do to inherit eternal life?'" (Mark 10:17)

"Inherit eternal life" is another way of saying "enter the kingdom of God" or "have treasure in heaven" or "be saved". All these phrases are used in Mark 10 to mean a similar thing: the overwhelming joy of being forgiven and accepted by God himself, free to enjoy him forever – in this life, and the life to come. "What must I do," says the man, "to get that? How can I be good enough?"

Jesus asks a question straight back.

"'Why do you call me good?' Jesus answered. 'No one is good – except God alone.'" (Mark 10:18)

Jesus offers the man a reality check: how good is good enough for God?

We tend to think of ourselves as basically good because we usually only compare ourselves to other people. It's easy to puff ourselves up like a balloon if we only see ourselves in relation to certain people on TV, or people we don't like.

But Jesus is saying, "If you want to know who really deserves to be called good, who really deserves to inherit eternal life, try comparing yourself to God – who alone is perfectly just, perfectly wise, perfectly pure and perfectly loving. Then you'll get a sense of how good you really are."

But the man doesn't get it. So Jesus continues.

"'You know the commandments: "Do not murder, do not commit adultery, do not steal, do not give false testimony, do not defraud, honour your father and mother."'

"'Teacher,' he declared, 'all these I have kept since I was a boy.'" (Mark 10:19-20)

If God were to say to this man, "Why should I give you eternal life?", that's the answer the man would give:

"I've kept all your commands since I was a boy."

But has he? Jesus, gently and lovingly, gives this man a second reality check:

"Jesus looked at him and loved him. 'One thing you lack,' he said. 'Go, sell everything you have and give to the poor, and you will have treasure in heaven. Then come, follow me.'" (Mark 10:21)

Has the man really kept all the commands? Is he even keeping what Jesus calls the first and most important command, to love the Lord your God with all your heart, soul, mind and strength? To see if he really does love God like that, Jesus tests the man with a challenge:

Give your money away.

It reminds me of the famous story. A robber goes up to a rich man, points a gun at him and says, "Your money or your life". But the rich man says nothing. So the robber shouts louder: "I'm not kidding – your money or your life!" And the man says, "I'm thinking, I'm thinking!"

Money or life. It should be a no-brainer. But what will the rich man choose?

"At this the man's face fell. He went away sad, because he had great wealth." (Mark 10:22)

Faced with the choice between keeping his money or gaining eternal life, this man chooses money. The fact that he walks away from Jesus at this point shows that – although he thinks of himself as a good person – in reality, money is more important to him than God.

It also shows that he didn't see the danger he was in. If the building you're in is on fire, you don't stop to fill your hands with your valuables. Your life is more important than that.

I wonder what it would be for us. What is the one thing you would not be willing to let go of, in order to gain the eternal life that Jesus offers? Our answer to that question reveals how far we are from good, and how far we are from God.

"Jesus looked around and said to his disciples, 'How hard it is for the rich to enter the kingdom of God!'

"The disciples were amazed at his words. But Jesus said again, 'Children, how hard

it is to enter the kingdom of God! It is easier for a camel to go through the eye of a needle than for a rich man to enter the kingdom of God.'" (Mark 10:23-25)

In other words, it's impossible. The disciples were amazed because money was seen as a blessing from God; they understood it to mean that God was pleased with a person. But Jesus is saying that even a morally upright, thoroughly religious, politically powerful, exceedingly wealthy young man can never do enough good things to get to heaven. Those good deeds are all just a lot of hot air. Why?

Because nothing we do, nothing we are, can change the fact that deep down, all of us have a serious heart problem that separates us from God.

As we've already seen, Jesus exposes the real state of our hearts when he says:

"What comes out of a man is what makes him 'unclean.' For from within, out of men's hearts, come evil thoughts, sexual immorality, theft, murder, adultery, greed, malice, deceit, lewdness, envy, slander, arrogance and folly. All these evils come from inside and make a man 'unclean.'" (Mark 7:20-23)

It is what we are. Deep down at the very core of our being.

When I was young, I went on a rugby tour, and while we were travelling I got this awful skin disease which made my face look not unlike a cheese and tomato pizza. So I started putting Band-Aids on my face, little sticky plasters to cover up these horrible sores that made people sick at the sight of me. Now, the plasters helped to cover up the fact that something was wrong with me, but of course they were powerless to cure the disease. For that, the doctor had to prescribe some industrial strength antibiotics to get at the infection deep in my blood stream.

In the same way, the things we do to try and make ourselves good enough are like sticking plasters or Band-Aids. They may cover up the fact that there's a problem deep down in our hearts. They may make other people think we're pretty good people. We may even fool ourselves.

But the things we do are completely powerless to cure the problem of our sin. Any answer that begins, "God, you should give me eternal life because I…" – any answer which places confidence in anything you are or anything you have done – will not be of any use. Again, let me say as clearly as I can that according to Jesus, these things will do you no good at all when it comes to inheriting eternal life. If you're putting your trust in any of these things, please don't, because you've been misled.

Now, it's not that these are bad things to do. They're very good things to do.

But they become bad if we're trusting in them to earn eternal life for us; if we're using them to try and justify ourselves in God's eyes.

Jesus' words quickly bring the rich young man down to earth. Regardless of how moral or good we think we are, we fail to obey even the very first command, the most important command: love the Lord your God with all your heart, soul, mind and strength. Like the man, our hearts love other things more – and that is what separates us from God.

The disciples understand immediately that this leaves all of us in a desperate situation. If a rich man can't make it into the kingdom of God, then who on earth can?

"The disciples were even more amazed, and said to each other, 'Who then can be saved?'" (Mark 10:26)

And Jesus' answer is devastating.

"Jesus looked at them and said, 'With man this is impossible…'"

In other words, there are some things we will never deserve, can never earn, and should never even try to pay for.

But that doesn't mean we can't receive it as a gift from God. Jesus continues:

"With man this is impossible, but not with God; all things are possible with God." (Mark 10:27)

So how can anyone inherit eternal life if there is nothing we can do to inherit it? Strangely enough, if the rich young man had arrived only a short while earlier, he would have heard Jesus answer exactly that question.

Immediately before this encounter, Jesus meets some people who are the opposite of the rich young man. Where he has material things, they have nothing. Where he is well respected, they are overlooked. He has power, but they are so weak they have to be brought to Jesus. And where he walks away sadly from Jesus, they cling to him.

"People were bringing little children to Jesus to have him touch them, but the disciples rebuked them. When Jesus saw this, he was indignant. He said to them, 'Let the little children come to me, and do not hinder them, for the kingdom of God belongs to such as these. I tell you the truth, anyone who will not receive the kingdom of God like a little child will never enter it.' And he took the children in his arms,

put his hands on them and blessed them." (Mark 10:13-16)

By speaking of little children, Jesus isn't saying we have to be naive or gullible to inherit the kingdom of God. And he isn't talking about innocence or purity here. Having been one myself, innocence is not a quality I'd associate with a little child.

The quality that little children have that Jesus commends is their dependency. They depend on someone else to do everything for them, because they know they can do nothing for themselves. All they can do is throw out their arms and cry for help.

Small children don't try and pay for their meals, or a place to sleep, or the love that their parents show them, because they can't. They have no way of paying. They are totally dependent, so they receive all of it as a gift.

Now all this makes the message of Jesus very different from other religions. Other faiths say if you do certain things, and don't do other things, then God will accept you.

But Jesus tells us that that is simply not true. Because the problem of the human heart is so serious, the only way we can ever hope to be accepted by God is if he reaches out to us, pays the price for our sin himself, and then offers us forgiveness as a gift. And that is exactly what happened when he sent Jesus to die on the cross in our place.

We can't earn it and we don't deserve it. In fact, we deserve the opposite – God's punishment. And yet Jesus took that punishment on our behalf, so that all those who put their trust in him would be freely forgiven.

If you want to enter the kingdom of God, says Jesus, if you want to experience the overwhelming joy of being forgiven and accepted by God himself, welcomed into the intimacy of his own family, free to enjoy him forever – in this life, and the life to come – if you want that, the only way to do it is to accept it as a child would accept it: knowing you have no way of earning it or deserving it, content simply to receive it joyfully as a gift.

All we can do is come to him – not with hands filled with all the things we have done, but with empty hands, ready to receive what God has done.

"God made him who had no sin to be sin for us, so that in him we might become the righteousness of God." (2 Corinthians 5:21)

In other words, Jesus took upon himself all our sin, so that we might take upon ourselves his righteousness. When God looks at us – if we've put our trust in Jesus – he sees the perfect obedience, the perfect righteousness of his Son.

And that is grace: God offering us a righteousness we don't deserve, cannot earn, and shouldn't try to pay for. It's something that must simply be received. It's not a reward, it's a gift – paid for by God himself.

When someone who doesn't know you tells you you're valuable, it might be nice, but that feeling won't last very long. When a spouse or a best friend who knows you well tells you how precious you are to them, it means the world. But when the Creator of the universe, who knows your heart inside-out, shows you that he would die for you, it changes everything.

It shows that although we're more sinful than we ever realized, we're more loved than we ever dreamed. It means we no longer need to pretend we're something we're not, because God knows all about our hearts, and still loves us anyway.

It also means we are freed from the slavery of constantly trying to get our sense of value from all the places we usually try to get it: money or power, religiousness or career, good looks or the approval of others. The reason we look to those things for our sense of self-worth is because we are not receiving it from God.

But when you come to Jesus, you understand just how valuable you are to God. When you look at the cross it's as if Jesus is saying, "This is what it costs to earn that gift for you. This is how serious your sin really is. And this is how much I love you anyway." We are more sinful than we ever realized, but more loved than we ever dreamed.

And that is the gift your Creator is holding out to you now.

"Come to me with empty hands," says Jesus. "There's something I want you to have."

Video – Day away I: The sower

["There are six exits on this plane… Four doors, two on each side… And two window exits over the wings. Each door has…"]

So far, we've explored who Jesus is and why Jesus came. The question now is, how should we respond? What does Jesus ask of us?

Early in Mark's Gospel we saw people coming to John the Baptist to have their sins forgiven.

They came out to him because they knew they were not the people they wanted to be, let alone the people God wanted them to be.

But John told them that someone much more powerful would come after him. Someone who would not only forgive their sin, but fill them with God's Holy Spirit.

As we'll see, in Mark chapter 4, Jesus in effect says: "If you come to me, it will be truly and miraculously life-changing. But you have to listen to me for that to happen."

In Mark chapter 4, Jesus tells a story that pictures the extraordinary, life-changing power of his words as tiny, vulnerable seeds.

What Jesus is saying is this. Just as seeds will only grow if you plant them properly, so the good news about me will only change your life… if you hear it properly.

"'Listen! A farmer went out to sow his seed. As he was scattering the seed, some fell along the path, and the birds came and ate it up. Some fell on rocky places, where it did not have much soil. It sprang up quickly, because the soil was shallow. But when the sun came up, the plants were scorched, and they withered because they had no root. Other seed fell among thorns, which grew up and choked the plants, so that they did not bear grain. Still other seed fell on good soil. It came up, grew and produced a crop, multiplying thirty, sixty, or even a hundred times.'

"Then Jesus said, 'He who has ears to hear, let him hear.'" (Mark 4:3-9)

I don't know if you realized it, but you had a walk-on part in that story. Everyone who has ever heard the good news, the gospel about Jesus, appears in it. It's as if Jesus is holding up a mirror so we can see ourselves reflected back.

You see, although this story is called "The Parable of the Sower", the main focus is not on the sower. Or the seed.

Jesus focuses on the soil. Because each one of us is a different kind of soil. Each one of us receives the good news about Jesus in a different way.

We know this because Jesus explains the parable to the disciples after he tells it. And he wants us to ask ourselves the question, how am I responding to the gospel? What kind of soil am I?

The first type of soil is in verse 4: the path, where the soil is hard. The seed falls on it, and the birds immediately come and eat it up. Jesus explains that some people, as they hear the good news about Jesus, are just like that hardened path:

"As soon as they hear it, Satan comes and takes away the word that was sown in them." (Mark 4:15)

The fields in ancient Israel were long, narrow strips divided by little paths. Over the years, the constant traffic of footsteps, hooves and wheels turned these paths as hard as concrete. So if seeds fell here, they'd never go deep into the soil, they'd just bounce off and remain on the surface.

The seed would become food for birds. Jesus says the birds who come and snatch up the seed are a picture of Satan, whose aim is always to stop the gospel from being properly heard – immediately if possible.

There's a sign near where I live. It says, "Thieves operate in this area. You don't have to be a victim. Guard your valuables."

And it's a very similar warning to the one Jesus gives here.

Satan is a reality, warns Jesus. He's like a thief who wants to take, not the wallet from your back pocket, but the gospel from your ears.

And there's nothing worse than discovering you've been robbed without knowing it. You don't even realize that you're missing something until much later.

But that's what happens here. Before the gospel even registers in the person's mind, something comes to snatch it away. This person may be a hardened skeptic who immediately rejects anything that will challenge their own ideas, or it may simply be someone who is easily distracted. As soon as the Bible is closed, the words are forgotten.

But, as the rest of the parable makes clear, you don't have to be a victim.

The second type of soil is in verse 5: the rocky places, where the soil is shallow.

"Others, like seed sown on rocky places, hear the word and at once receive it with joy. But since they have no root, they last only a short time. When trouble or persecution comes because of the word, they quickly fall away." (Mark 4:16-17)

In Israel, some of the land has a thin two or three-inch layer of soil lying on top of the limestone bedrock. If seed falls there, the sun heats the soil quickly because it's so shallow, and the seed immediately responds. In the short run, this soil looks like the best kind of soil. The immediate growth is spectacular. But the bedrock only a few inches below means there's nothing for the roots to go down into, and no way for the plant to get moisture. So it quickly dies.

I love books, but I have a terrible habit of starting one, getting into it, and then leaving it unfinished while I start another one.

Some people have the same issue with the gospel. They start with real eagerness. They seem truly excited about getting to know Christ. But then the early excitement fades.

Because of their interest in Jesus, friends, family and people at work start cutting them out of the conversation, keeping them at arm's length – or worse. And at that point, the person decides it's easier to give up on Jesus than put up with the discomfort. The Christian life gets discarded. They haven't thought through what it means to follow him, the cost of being for what he is for, and against what he is against. Their desire to know him is revealed as shallow and short-lived, and they're not grounded enough to persevere, to finish what they started.

The third type of soil is in verse 7, and this soil has thorns that choke whatever the soil produces. Jesus explains:

"Still others, like seed sown among thorns, hear the word; but the worries of this life, the deceitfulness of wealth and the desires for other things come in and choke the word, making it unfruitful." (Mark 4:18-19)

At first the plant seems to be doing well. But it can't compete with the thorns which grow up alongside it.

It's like the story of the young man who said, "Darling, I want you to know that I love you more than anything else in the world. Will you marry me? I know I'm not rich, I don't have a big house or a beautiful car like Jeffrey Brown, but I do love you with all my heart." And the young woman replies, "I love you with all my heart too, but tell me more about Jeffrey Brown."

It's the same for the third type of person in the parable. Somehow they let their desire for other things become competition for their involvement with Jesus.

Their hearts are divided. Desire for security, comfort, approval or power, maybe money, maybe the desire for a potential spouse who doesn't share their view of Jesus – these desires, and the worries that come with them, become stronger than the desire for Jesus.

This person doesn't see that the security, comfort, approval and power that come from knowing Christ infinitely outweigh any treasure the world has to offer.

But the fourth and final type of soil is in verse 8: the good soil that produces a vast crop. Jesus explains:

"Others, like seed sown on good soil, hear the word, accept it, and produce a crop – thirty, sixty or even a hundred times what was sown." (Mark 4:20)

This type of growth is out of the ordinary. Even modern farming methods can't produce the kind of huge crop Jesus describes here. He wants us to understand that something supernatural is happening.

When the gospel is heard by someone who truly hears it and does what it says, something miraculous happens, something that cannot be accounted for in human terms. And it happens when the person hearing the gospel sees Jesus for who he is, understands why he came, and what it means to follow him. It happens when they understand that Jesus is the greatest treasure in the world.

When I was younger I used to get a comic delivered by mail. It always arrived on a Tuesday just after breakfast, but because I had to go to school, I didn't get a chance to read it until break time. And when that moment came I used to run out and find somewhere I wouldn't be disturbed.

Nothing could be allowed to stop me from reading that week's edition of my favourite comic.

Now, the surroundings weren't the most comfortable, but I was completely content as I opened my bag to read my comic. Nothing else mattered. Why? Because I had my treasure. It was all I wanted or needed.

When Jesus talks about the fourth kind of soil in this parable, he's talking about someone who not only hears the gospel about Jesus Christ, but makes it their treasure. When Jesus himself becomes more valuable to you than anything else in the world, that's when you know you've really heard him.

There may be areas of your heart you think are impenetrable and unreachable. There may be self-image issues, battles with addiction or alienation or abuse. You may feel trapped by all kinds of darkness inside you, things you feel you can't even admit. Let this parable give you hope.

I remember the story of a man who visited a cemetery in Italy. He said he noticed a thick marble slab over the top of one of the graves.

But, somehow, about a hundred years earlier, an acorn had fallen through a small crack into the grave. And over the years the acorn had grown and grown until eventually it had smashed through the surface of the hard marble and cracked the enormous slab into two pieces. As the tree grew up, it just pushed the marble aside as if it wasn't there.

There's a lot of power packed in that seed. All it needed was the right kind of soil. The good news about Jesus, though it may seem small and weak, has the power to break through any human heart – if only we will listen and act on what we hear.

The word of God doesn't come to us so that we can give the right answers to religious questions. It comes to us because God wants us to be in relationship with him. The gospel tells us that Jesus Christ has fully paid the price for sin on the cross, so the way is now open for us to know God and enjoy him forever, if only we will trust him.

But Jesus wouldn't have told the parable if that was an easy thing to do.

It's not a passive thing. It's not something that will just happen regardless of whether or not we choose to act on what we hear.

Jesus in effect says: "I can change your life. But are you listening?"

Video – Day away II: James and John

If God said to you, "What do you want me to do for you?" what would you ask for?

What are the things that, for you, make life worth living? What do you find yourself daydreaming about most? What are the things that – if you couldn't have them – would make you feel your life was empty and pointless?

In Mark chapter 10, two of Jesus' disciples – James and John – tell Jesus exactly what they want from him. And under the circumstances, their words couldn't be any more inappropriate.

But first, before James and John tell Jesus what they want from him, Jesus tells James and John what he is going to do for them.

"'We are going up to Jerusalem,' he said, 'and the Son of Man will be betrayed to the chief priests and teachers of the law. They will condemn him to death and will hand him over to the Gentiles, who will mock him and spit on him, flog him and kill him. Three days later he will rise.'" (Mark 10:33-34)

So how will James and John respond to the news that their closest friend of the past three years is about to be brutally murdered? Grief? Greed.

"Then James and John ... came to him. 'Teacher,' they said, 'we want you to do for us whatever we ask.'

"'What do you want me to do for you?' he asked.

"They replied, 'Let one of us sit at your right and the other at your left in your glory.'" (Mark 10:35-37)

Although they've just called Jesus "teacher", there's clearly something about Jesus' teaching they haven't yet understood.

He is deliberately going to give up his life for others. They, on the other hand, are desperately trying to hang on to their lives for themselves. And this is not the first time the disciples have revealed a petty, small-minded lust for glory.

Three times in Mark's Gospel, Jesus tells his disciples that he must suffer, die and rise again. And the incredible thing is that on two occasions, the disciples' react by thinking of their own greatness.

They want power and prestige. They want importance and status and recognition. Like many of us, they want to win. But Jesus wants something different for them. Something infinitely better.

"'You don't know what you are asking,' Jesus said. 'Can you drink the cup I drink or be baptized with the baptism I am baptized with?'" (Mark 10:38)

Now what Jesus means here is: Can you do what I will do?

Can you die on behalf of sinners? Can you bring down the barrier separating sinful human beings from their Creator once and for all, so that they can have an infinitely satisfying relationship with God? And can you be raised to life again to prove that death and sin have been conquered?

"'We can,' they answered." (Mark 10:39)

But of course, they can't.

Like you and me, James and John need to be saved themselves from God's rightful anger at sin. As Jesus said, they don't know what they're asking.

They're blind to the fact that the joy of following Jesus isn't found in status. It's found in service.

When the other disciples find out what James and John have been saying to Jesus, we read that they "became indignant" with them. And let's be honest, that's not because they think James and John were wrong to ask for power. It's because they wish they'd thought of it first.

"Jesus called them together and said, 'You know that those who are regarded as rulers of the Gentiles lord it over them, and their high officials exercise authority over them.'" (Mark 10:42)

That's the way of the world. And it's the way of James and John. We try to grasp for power so that we can lord it over other people. But now listen to the way Jesus turns things upside down.

"Not so with you. Instead, whoever wants to become great among you must be your servant, and whoever wants to be first must be slave of all." (Mark 10:43-44)

Jesus says, "If you're really my disciples, everything's got to change. If you really want to be first in the kingdom of God, if you really want to win, get ready to serve."

But why would anyone want to trade in status for service? How can we possibly loosen our grip on the things that we want so badly?

The reason James and John and the other disciples are grasping after these things is because they don't understand that Jesus is already offering them something infinitely more valuable. Himself.

"Even the Son of Man did not come to be served, but to serve, and to give his life as a ransom for many." (Mark 10:45)

You see, if Jesus had simply given them what they wanted, it never would have satisfied them anyway. No amount of power, or money, or achievement, or family, or friendship, or sex or spirituality is ever enough in itself. We just want more.

And there's a reason for that. The deepest cravings we have – the ones that we unsuccessfully try to fill with all these other things – can only be fully satisfied by loving and serving the One who made us. It's the way he made us to be.

We go looking for contentment and satisfaction and fulfilment in all the wrong places, and we chase after them in the hope that they'll give us what only God can.

In the Bible, it's called idolatry: turning something God has created into a substitute for God. It's turning a good thing… into a God thing.

And Jesus' closest disciples do it, even when Jesus has just personally offered them the greatest treasure in the entire universe.

The writer C. S. Lewis once said:

"We are half-hearted creatures, fooling about with drink and sex and ambition when infinite joy is offered us, like an ignorant child who wants to go on making mud pies in a slum because he cannot imagine what is meant by the offer of a holiday at the sea. We are far too easily pleased."

That's James and John. That's us. Far too easily pleased. If only we had eyes to see it.

But Mark chapter 10 ends with real hope. Because there, ironically enough, is a blind man with perfect vision.

"As Jesus and his disciples, together with a large crowd, were leaving the city, a blind man, Bartimaeus … was sitting by the roadside begging. When he heard that it was Jesus of Nazareth, he began to shout, 'Jesus, Son of David, have mercy on me!'" (Mark 10:46-47)

Bartimaeus is different from the disciples in many ways. Apart from the fact of his physical blindness, he's a beggar who has nothing of any material value apart from his cloak. He doesn't call Jesus "teacher", but "Son of David" – in other words, God's King in God's world. It's the only place in Mark that someone recognizes Jesus in this way.

And notice that, rather than coming to Jesus with a demand that Jesus should do for him whatever he asks, Bartimaeus knows he deserves nothing, has nothing to offer, and simply cries out for mercy.

"Many rebuked him and told him to be quiet, but he shouted all the more, 'Son of David, have mercy on me!'" (Mark 10:48)

Unlike the disciples who care about their own status, Bartimaeus is willing to make a fool of himself in the eyes of others, so long as he is able to get close to Jesus.

"Jesus stopped and said, 'Call him.' So they called to the blind man, 'Cheer up! On your feet! He's calling you.'

"Throwing his cloak aside, he jumped to his feet and came to Jesus." (Mark 10:49-50)

The cloak is all he has of any material value. But he lets it fall to the ground, because he knows that standing right in front of him there is something – or someone – of infinitely greater value.

"'What do you want me to do for you?' Jesus asked him.

"The blind man said, 'Rabbi, I want to see.'" (Mark 10:51)

To Bartimaeus, Jesus is more than just a "teacher". He uses a word that in the original language means "Master". "Master", he says, "I want to see."

And that, ironically, is exactly the request James and John should have made.

"'Go,' said Jesus, 'your faith has healed you.'

"Immediately he received his sight and followed Jesus along the road." (Mark 10:52)

James and John and Bartimaeus are asked exactly the same question by Jesus: "What do you want me to do for you?" And isn't it striking that while the disciples are rebuked by Jesus for their request, Bartimaeus is "healed" – a word which literally means "saved".

Why does Jesus respond differently? Because while the disciples demand that Jesus do whatever they ask of him, Bartimaeus knows he's in no position to make demands. He knows he needs mercy.

Although James and John are blind to it, blind Bartimaeus knows that the greatest treasure in the entire universe is standing right in front of him. He knows it can't be grabbed with a grasping fist.

All he can do is open up his hand, beg for mercy, and begin to follow Jesus.

So how should we respond to Jesus?

What do you want him to do for you?

Video – Day away III: Herod

Ignoring your conscience can be a terrible thing. As the old saying goes, "we are the choices we have made".

Conscience is a nag. It tells us to do inconvenient things at inconvenient times, it makes us uncomfortable and it won't leave us in peace.

But sometimes, listening to our conscience – and by that I mean our God-given sense of right and wrong – will affect far more than our bodies. It will affect the ultimate destiny of our souls. Because we are the choices that we have made.

Mark chapter 6 contains one of the darkest moments in the Bible. It records the story of King Herod Antipas, the ruler of Galilee, a man who tragically refused to listen to his conscience, even though it cost a man his life... and may well have cost him his own.

Also caught up in the tragedy is John the Baptist, a man we were introduced to at the very beginning of Mark's Gospel.

A friendless, solitary figure, John the Baptist tells people about Jesus and the rescue he offers. He urges people to "repent", a word which means to turn away from sin, and turn back to God.

And that's exactly the kind of talk that can get you into serious trouble.

"Herod ... had given orders to have John arrested, and he had him bound and put in prison.

"He did this because of Herodias, his brother Philip's wife, whom he had married. For John had been saying to Herod, 'It is not lawful for you to have your brother's wife.' So Herodias nursed a grudge against John and wanted to kill him. But she was not able to, because Herod feared John and protected him, knowing him to be a righteous and holy man. When Herod heard John, he was greatly puzzled; yet he liked to listen to him." (Mark 6:17-20)

Before he met Herodias, Herod had been married for over twenty years. However, during a visit to Rome he allowed himself to fall in love with Herodias, his brother's wife. Herod proposed to her and she agreed to leave her husband, as long as Herod agreed to leave his wife.

So they started living together in Galilee. And even though John the Baptist tells Herod that what he is doing is wrong, and we know that Herod respects John as a "righteous and holy man" (Mark 6:20), Herod ignores the warning, and his own conscience. He puts John in prison, perhaps partly to protect him from Herodias, who wanted John dead because of what he'd been saying.

We're told that every time Herod heard John, he was "greatly puzzled". Now this doesn't mean that he was confused by John's teaching, as John's teaching was pretty clear. It means that Herod's morals were thrown into confusion, because John had exposed the way in which Herod was rebelling against God. Nevertheless, as we saw, Herod "liked to listen to him" (Mark 6:20).

Perhaps you've experienced something similar as you've come to see that you've been living life without reference to the loving Creator who made you. Perhaps, like Herod listening to John, you listen to the words of Jesus and want to go on listening, despite the disturbance they cause.

So Herod continued to listen. Week after week it went on. The people at the palace must have thought that their king had gone religious.

Mark tells us that "Herod feared John", even to the extent of protecting him. But there was something that Herod was not prepared to do.

Yes, he would listen. Yes, he acknowledged that John was a good man. Yes, he was even prepared to give John his protection. But Herod would not stop his adultery. He would not turn away from what he knew was wrong. Or as the Bible puts it, he would not repent.

As we've seen, the right response when we understand that we have been rebelling against God is to repent. It is to do an about-turn, to turn away from our rebellion and come to God for forgiveness and rescue. But that's the one thing Herod won't do.

Then one day, on his birthday, Herod throws a party for all his friends and colleagues. Mark's comment at this point is very striking: "Finally the opportune time came" (Mark 6:21).

As we're about to see, it's an opportune time for Herod, but also for Herodias. The question is: who will seize the opportunity, and who will miss it?

"On his birthday Herod gave a banquet for his high officials and military commanders and the leading men of Galilee.

"When the daughter of Herodias came in and danced, she pleased Herod and his dinner guests." (Mark 6:21-22)

In other words, Herodias' daughter dances in a way that gets the half-drunk guests sexually aroused. Herod, in a phrase designed to impress upon his guests what a generous, powerful man he is, says to the girl:

"'Ask me for anything you want, and I'll give it to you.' And he promised her with an oath, 'Whatever you ask I will give you, up to half my kingdom.'" (Mark 6:22-23)

"She went out and said to her mother, 'What shall I ask for?'" (Mark 6:24)

And Herodias doesn't need to be asked twice.

"At once the girl hurried in to the king with the request: 'I want you to give me right now the head of John the Baptist on a platter.'" (Mark 6:25)

And this is the key moment in Herod's life. He is suddenly in an extremely dangerous place. We are the choices we make. And this choice – this moment – will have a profound effect on what Herod will become. Will he stand up for what he knows is right, or will he suppress his conscience one more time?

"The king was greatly distressed, but because of his oaths and his dinner guests, he did not want to refuse her. So he immediately sent an executioner with orders to bring John's head. The man went, beheaded John in the prison, and brought back his head on a platter. He presented it to the girl, and she gave it to her mother." (Mark 6:26-28)

Under pressure from friends, family and work colleagues, Herod stopped listening to his conscience. He allowed the head that warned him, the tongue that told him to repent and be rescued, to be literally cut off.

Much as he feared John, Herod feared his guests more.

And when all is said and done, I wonder if Herod's guests really did respect him any the more for keeping his drunken oaths, and needlessly slaughtering a man he had previously protected?

But how many of us would have done a similar thing in Herod's position? The fact remains that many, many people will do just that. At the crucial moment, we will deny what we know is right because of what the family will think, what business colleagues may do, or because of what friends will say. Or because we know it will mean changing much-loved habits.

It's no small thing when we consider what we have to lose if we obey Jesus' words.

Jesus himself knew first-hand what it was like to suffer, to be misunderstood and ridiculed – even by his own family. In Mark chapter 3, we read that his family:

"…went to take charge of him, for they said, 'He is out of his mind.'" (Mark 3:21)

But when his family arrive at the house where he is teaching, Jesus says something remarkable.

"A crowd was sitting around him, and they told him, 'Your mother and brothers are outside looking for you.'

"'Who are my mother and my brothers?' he asked.

"Then he looked at those seated in a circle around him and said, 'Here are my mother and my brothers! Whoever does God's will is my brother and sister and mother.'" (Mark 3:32-35)

It may be that in listening to your conscience, you feel afraid of what it will cost you to do what you know is right. I hope Jesus' words here are a great comfort. He reminds us that if we take his words seriously, even if the people closest to you think you're out of your mind, there is a loving family of fellow believers who are there to support and encourage one another. Whoever does God's will, whoever follows Jesus, is your brother and sister and mother.

But it goes even further than that. In Mark chapter 10, Jesus makes this amazing promise to all those who put their trust in him:

"'I tell you the truth,' Jesus replied, 'no one who has left home or brothers or sisters or mother or father or children or fields for me and the gospel will fail to re-

ceive a hundred times as much in this present age (homes, brothers, sisters, mothers, children and fields – and with them, persecutions) and in the age to come, eternal life.'" (Mark 10:29-30)

Yes, there will be persecutions of one kind or another. But with them, Jesus promises extraordinary blessings, and extraordinary joy, that will far outweigh any suffering we might face.

I wonder if you see the parallels Mark wants us to draw between John the Baptist and Jesus? Both preached the same message – that we need to turn from our rebellion against God and accept the rescue he has lovingly provided.

Both were protected by powerful men: Herod and Pontius Pilate, both of whom tried to remain neutral but could not. And both John and Jesus suffered violent deaths as a result.

There is, of course, one further point of comparison. Why were both John and Jesus killed? Because in both cases, when Herod and Pilate found themselves under pressure from those around them, they would not listen to their conscience.

Herod is mentioned a final time in the Gospels. Pontius Pilate sends Jesus to meet Herod, and in Luke chapter 23, Luke records what happened. The meeting between Herod and Jesus is ominous, not because of what is said, but because of what is not said. Luke tells us:

"When Herod saw Jesus, he was greatly pleased, because for a long time he had been wanting to see him. From what he had heard about him, he hoped to see him perform some miracle. He plied him with many questions, but Jesus gave him no answer." (Luke 23:8-9)

You see, there does come a time, after repeatedly refusing to repent, when sadly there is no longer an opportunity to do so. It's easy to put it off, to say that we don't have time, or to think that we have too much to lose, or that there'll be a more convenient time in the future.

Of course, it's never easy to repent. And conscience is rarely convenient. But Herod's story reminds us that there is a cost when we refuse to listen to God's word. It also warns us that we may not get an opportunity later.

When Herod got no answer from Jesus, he and his soldiers mocked Jesus by dressing him in an elegant robe and sending him back to Pilate, who apparently enjoyed the joke. We read that on that day:

"Herod and Pilate became friends – before this they had been enemies" (Luke 23:12).

It is a tragedy that John the Baptist lost his life. But the tragedy of Herod himself is even greater. Because when he silenced his own conscience, he lost something that was more precious even than life itself: the opportunity to turn away from his wrongdoing and turn back to God. The opportunity to repent.

Ignoring Jesus' call to repent and believe may earn us the approval of other people.

It may even win us friends.

But it will eventually earn us the rejection of Jesus.

Video Episode 7: Come and die

Your eyes sometimes have a funny way of playing tricks on you.

For example, what do you see when you look at this picture?

There are actually two women here: an old woman and a young woman. Not everyone can see both. If you can't see them, try looking at the old woman's chin here... or the young woman's chin here.

If you still can't see them, they are there. Trust me, I'm a Christian.

But I wonder what you've seen as you've looked at the picture of Jesus in Mark's Gospel? Because in a similar way, as we look at Jesus, there are two aspects to his identity, two faces to be seen at the same time. There's the human face of Jesus, but there's also the divine face of Christ. And not everyone can see both.

Some of us, just like the disciples, can stare at the face of Jesus for years – and all we can see is the man. Like the disciples in Mark's Gospel, it's possible to spend lots of time in Jesus' company, and yet be totally blind to the divine face of Christ.

Well, what did the disciples see when they looked at him?

They saw an apparently uneducated man who taught as no one had ever taught. They saw a man who cured incurable diseases. A man who could control nature with a word. A man who took the hand of a corpse and raised it to life. A man who demonstrated authority to forgive sin.

They saw him do all these things. They ask themselves in Mark chapter 4, "Who is this?". And yet incredibly, they are still blind to the answer Jesus has been giving them all along. By the time we get to Mark chapter 8, Jesus is exasperated with them. He says:

"Do you still not see or understand? Are your hearts hardened? Do you have eyes but fail to see, and ears but fail to hear?" (Mark 8:17-18)

If being a first-hand witness of all these staggering events is not enough to make them see who Jesus is, then what hope is there? Who can possibly cure that kind of blindness?

And then, as if to answer that question, Jesus gives a blind man his sight. But this healing is unique. It's the only one that happens gradually.

"They came to Bethsaida, and some people brought a blind man and begged Jesus to touch him. He took the blind man by the hand and led him outside the village. When he had spit on the man's eyes and put his hands on him, Jesus asked, 'Do you see anything?'

"He looked up and said, 'I see people; they look like trees walking around.'

"Once more Jesus put his hands on the man's eyes. Then his eyes were opened, his sight was restored, and he saw everything clearly." (Mark 8:22-25)

First, Jesus touches the blind man, and he begins to see, but only partially. Then, Jesus touches him again, and this time the man sees everything clearly.

Just like the optical illusion. It's a reminder that sometimes, even when we think we can see, actually we can only see part of the picture.

And now we reach a turning point in Mark's Gospel. Will the disciples finally be able to see who Jesus is?

"Jesus and his disciples went on to the villages around Caesarea Philippi. On the way he asked them, 'Who do people say I am?'

"They replied, 'Some say John the Baptist; others say Elijah; and still others, one of the prophets.'

"'But what about you?' he asked. 'Who do you say I am?'" (Mark 8:27-29)

Jesus suddenly asks them a very personal question here, and this is where it gets very personal for us, too. Can we only see the human face of Jesus, or can we also see the divine face of Christ? Who do we say Jesus is? Teacher? Healer? Miracle Worker?

"Peter answered, 'You are the Christ.'" (Mark 8:29)

Finally, Peter sees it. Or does he?

"Jesus warned them not to tell anyone about him." (Mark 8:30)

You see, Jesus knows the disciples' blindness is only partly cured. Although they can see who he is, they don't yet see why he's come – or what it means to follow him.

That's why Jesus immediately begins to teach them more about himself. It's as if he's starting to correct their partial vision.

"He then began to teach them that the Son of Man must suffer many things and be rejected by the elders, chief priests and teachers of the law, and that he must be killed and after three days rise again." (Mark 8:31)

That's why Jesus came. He came to die and rise again. In fact, Jesus himself says he "must" die. He knows it's the only way sinful people like you and me can be brought back into a relationship with our loving Creator.

And now we reach the next turning point in Mark's Gospel. Peter has understood who Jesus is, but will he understand why Jesus came?

"Peter took him aside and began to re-buke him." (Mark 8:32)

Again, it gets very personal for us. Can we see not only who Jesus is, but why Jesus came? Do we understand how serious our sin is, and how badly we need rescue? Or, like Peter, does the idea of Jesus' death fill us only with horror and disgust?

If we're like Peter, Jesus has some very strong words for us at this point.

"When Jesus turned and looked at his dis-ciples, he rebuked Peter. 'Get behind me, Satan!' he said. 'You do not have in mind the things of God, but the things of men.'" (Mark 8:33)

If we have in mind the things of men, then Jesus' death on the cross seems pointless, tragic and weak. But seen in a different way, having in mind the things of God, there has never been a more powerful mo-ment in all of human history.

Although we don't deserve anything apart from his condemnation, and although he did not need to rescue any of us, yet in his amazing love, Jesus humbled himself by coming to earth, becoming a man, and suffering and dying for the very people who had been rebelling against him all their lives. He died for sinners, taking the punishment we deserve, so that we could enjoy the relationship with God that we were created to enjoy. Forever.

But there is one more thing the disciples need to understand before they see can see everything clearly. Because it's not enough to see who Jesus is. It's not even enough to see why he came. Just like the disciples, we also need to see what it means to follow him.

Jesus says that if we are his followers, we'll do two things. We'll deny ourselves, and take up our cross.

"Then he called the crowd to him along with his disciples and said: 'If anyone would come after me, he must deny him-self and take up his cross and follow me.'" (Mark 8:34)

The explorer Ernest Shackleton, when he was looking for people to go with him on his exploration of the Antarctic, reportedly placed an ad in a newspaper. It said simply:

"Men wanted for hazardous journey. Low wages, bitter cold, long hours of complete darkness. Safe return doubtful. Honour and recognition in event of success."

There is something of that in Jesus' call to each one of us. The message is: "Come and die." Following him will cost us a great deal: it may cost us in terms of relation-ships, careers, comfort, it may even – in some places – cost us our lives.

But there's a crucial difference between Shackleton's call, and Jesus' call. The dif-ference is that if we respond to Jesus' call, there is no doubt about the final outcome.

All the way through Mark's Gospel, Jesus has demonstrated ultimate power and au-thority over everything – sin, sickness, na-ture, even death itself. He has shown time and again his love, his mercy, his grace – even to the most broken, rejected people.

If we give our lives to him, it's not a suicidal gesture. In fact, it's the complete opposite. Listen to what Jesus says next:

"Whoever wants to save his life will lose it, but whoever loses his life for me and for the gospel will save it. What good is it for a man to gain the whole world, yet forfeit his soul? Or what can a man give in exchange for his soul? If anyone is ashamed of me and my words in this adulterous and sinful generation, the Son of Man will be ashamed of him when he comes in his Father's glory with the holy angels." (Mark 8:35-38)

You see, not only does Jesus have ultimate authority over sin, sickness, nature and death, he also has ultimate authority over us. If we try to save ourselves by rejecting Jesus, we will end up losing the very thing we're so desperate to hang on to.

If we really want to save our lives, we must entrust them to Jesus. And, having explored Mark's Gospel for ourselves, we can do that knowing we can trust him.

A true follower of Christ is someone who clearly sees what it will cost to follow him, but does it joyfully anyway, knowing that Jesus is worth infinitely more. Even more than friendship, or family, or career, even more than life itself.

What is given up is nothing compared to what is gained.

Immediately after this, in Mark chapter 9, some of the disciples witness something that once again demonstrates powerfully that Jesus can be trusted, that he is exactly who he says he is.

"After six days Jesus took Peter, James and John with him and led them up a high mountain, where they were all alone. There he was transfigured before them. His clothes became dazzling white, whiter than anyone in the world could bleach them. And there appeared before them Elijah and Moses, who were talking with Jesus." (Mark 9:2-4)

"Then a cloud appeared and enveloped them, and a voice came from the cloud: 'This is my Son, whom I love. Listen to him!'" (Mark 9:7)

Just as we saw in the very first chapter of Mark, God the Father tells us exactly who Jesus is: "This is my Son, whom I love."

But he also tells us how we should respond: "Listen to him!"

So as our journey through Mark's Gospel comes to an end, we're left with three questions:

What do you see when you look at Jesus? Is he just a good man, or is he the Christ, the Son of God?

What do you see when you look at his death? Was it just a tragic waste of a young life, or is it a rescue, a "ransom for many"?

And finally, what do you see as you consider Jesus' call? Is it a call to come and die?

Or can you see that because of his death and resurrection, he is calling you to come and die…

…and live.

ACKNOWLEDGEMENTS

Christianity Explored Handbooks

Authors	Barry Cooper, Craig Dyer, Alison Mitchell, Sam Shammas, Rico Tice
Editor	Alison Mitchell
Designer	André Parker

Christianity Explored Films

Director	Steve Hughes
Producer	Jane Hughes
Writer	Barry Cooper
Teacher	Rico Tice

Special Thanks

All those who've given such
helpful feedback over the years.

SUPPORTING DOWNLOADS FROM
WWW.CEMINISTRIES.ORG

When you register your course at **www.ceministries.org** you'll get free access to training modules, tips for setting up your course, talk outlines, visual aids, video trailers, book recommendations, and much more.

There's also a website designed exclusively for non-Christians, **www. christianityexplored.org**. You'll find videos answering tough questions, a visual outline explaining what Christianity is all about, and real-life stories from people who've started to follow Jesus.

Christianity Explored Ministries (CEM) aims to provide Christian churches and organisations worldwide with resources which explain the Christian faith clearly and relevantly from the Bible. CEM receives royalties from the sale of these resources, but is reliant on donations for the majority of its income. CEM is registered for charitable purposes in both the United Kingdom and the USA. **www.ceministries.org**

COURSES AVAILABLE FROM

CHRISTIANITY
EXPLORED
MINISTRIES

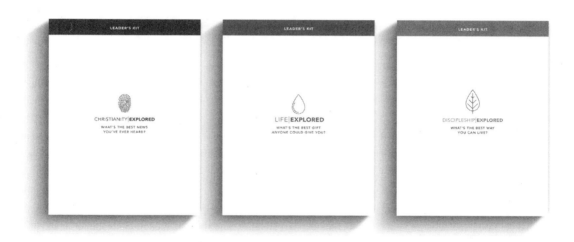

Leader's kits contain everything you need
to evaluate the course.

For more information visit
www.ceministries.org